The King v. Picariello and Lassandro

The King v. Picariello and Lassandro

BY GISELE AMANTEA

FRANK IACOBUCCI CENTRE FOR ITALIAN CANADIAN STUDIES
DEPARTMENT OF ITALIAN STUDIES | UNIVERSITY OF TORONTO

PUBLISHED BY THE FRANK IACOBUCCI CENTRE FOR ITALIAN CANADIAN STUDIES, DEPARTMENT OF ITALIAN STUDIES, UNIVERSITY OF TORONTO, IN CO-OPERATION WITH THE DUNLOP ART GALLERY, REGINA PUBLIC LIBRARY.

LIBRARY AND ARCHIVES CANADA CATALOGUING IN PUBLICATION

AMANTEA, GISELE
THE KING V. PICARIELLO AND LASSANDRO / GISELE AMANTEA.

ISBN 978-0-7727-8957-0

1. PICARIELLO, EMILIO, 1879-1923--TRIALS, LITIGATION, ETC.
2. LOSANDRO, FLORENCE, D. 1923--TRIALS, LITIGATION, ETC.
3. TRIALS (MURDER)--ALBERTA. 4. EXECUTIONS AND EXECUTIONERS--ALBERTA.
5. SMUGGLERS--ALBERTA. 6. PROHIBITION--ALBERTA--HISTORY--20TH CENTURY.
I. FRANK IACOBUCCI CENTRE FOR ITALIAN CANADIAN STUDIES II. TITLE.

KE229.P43A53 2007 364.152'309227123
C2007-900205-6

BOOK DESIGN
ZAB DESIGN & TYPOGRAPHY, WINNIPEG

PRINTED IN CANADA BY KROMAR

FOR JACK

Acknowledgments | Gisele Amantea

MY FATHER'S NAME IN ITS ENTIRETY was Serafino Givacehino Giovanni Casmir Amantea, but he was better known for most of his life as Jack. This is not the place to tell the stories about how his name shrank. Suffice it to say he was content being Jack and liked, thanks to the never ending childhood inquiries of my younger sister, to tell stories about growing up in Fernie in the first half of the twentieth century. When I reflect upon those circumstances and time I am filled with a kind of wonder. My father lived with marked personal tragedies and experienced prejudices that prevented him from going beyond the fifth grade in school. The latter also forced him and his first wife to elope. He was Italian Catholic and she was English Protestant. Later she would die as a relatively young woman, leaving my father with a teen-aged daughter to raise. My father was not an angry man, however, and he took great pride in both of his marriages and his immediate and large extended family. (His second marriage was to my mother, Jean — née Giannina Santopinto.) My father also lived through a period of remarkable technological and social transformation. His first car was a Model-T Ford and for most of his life his cultural homeland of Italy was regarded as virtually another planet in the solar system.

Despite the differences between that earlier era and our own, popular opinion and cultural stereotypes concerning immigration and race continue to be a source of bias and discrimination. Social justice is a constant in the story of *The King v. Picariello and Lassandro*. It is my hope that it reveals a parallel between this century and the last one and through the story of Emilio Picariello and Florence Lassandro invites consideration of how popular fiction and political agendas affect justice, history, and cultural perceptions, and how these impact individuals and cultural communities.

In addition to my late parents, I would like to acknowledge the critical role of numerous individuals and institutions in the creation of this book. I am pleased to thank Luca Somigli for his perceptive essay and the keen interest he has consistently shown in this work. Salvatore Bancheri, the director of the Frank Iacobucci Centre for Canadian Italian Studies, has been enthusiastic in administering the project. It has been an enriching experience to work with Elizabeth Hobart (Zab Design & Typography) and I am grateful to her for her efforts and creativity. I especially appreciate the Dunlop Art Gallery's unwavering support of this publication through a challenging time in the gallery's history. A number of past and present staff members worked to secure funding — Helen Marzolf, Donna Wawzonek, Annette Hurtig, and Elizabeth McLuhan. Concordia University Faculty of Fine Arts also contributed funding to the publication through a research grant and I am appreciative of the support of creative endeavours by members of the faculty. Joan Stebbins, Nancy Tousley, Will Straw, Johanne Sloan, Rosemary Donegan, and Patrick Traer offered valuable insight in the development of this work. Family members provided important information and assistance. They include Lucille Spina, Violet Minnifie, Rick and Shari Gris, and my sisters Jackie Kleiner and Gabrielle Enns. Finally my thanks go to Peter White, whose critical knowledge, love, and support continue to inspire my work.

Introduction | Luca Somigli

IN 1996 GISELE AMANTEA ASSEMBLED five haunting black and white works in an exhibition entitled *Requiescat* at the Stride Gallery in Calgary, Alberta. All five installations point, in different ways, to the vanishing of human presence: absent spectators, as in *and sorrow come near us no more* (1995), in which an empty armchair faces a switched-on television set; absent voices, as in *August the Sixteenth, 1984* (1993/94), a two-panel narrative, white handwriting on a black surface, unfolding from a line about Elvis Presley. Words and images thus seem to be merely the traces of an existence now departed as the title of the exhibition suggests. Indeed, the formula *requiescat in pace* lies on the threshold between presence and absence: spoken at funerals, it sanctions the disappearance of an individual into the repose of oblivion, while at the same time it entrusts to those who are left behind the memory of that missing presence. In the exhibition this play between presence and absence hinging on memory was powerfully caught in the narrative sequence of *August the Sixteenth, 1984*, in which the voice of an anonymous narrator recalls her Uncle Joe's funeral: "At the gravesite we are all standing around looking into a hole in the earth. They lower the casket into the ground, and suddenly a gust of wind blows dirt into my face stinging my eyes, like a bad omen. It was part of my uncle's life as a farmer. He tilled the soil to make the crops grow." The soil that will cover the casket is also, simultaneously, the trigger for a moment of recollection that brings Uncle Joe back to life, "his face all black and dirty after working in the fields," in the private chamber of the woman's memory.

If I approach Amantea's *The King v. Picariello and Lassandro* through such a circuitous route, it is because I see this book, and the art installation that preceded it, as growing out of the concerns with memory – with its power and pathos – already on display in the works collected in *Requiescat*. There the viewer was confronted by the private dimension of loss and remembrance. In *The King v. Picariello and Lassandro*, the same act of remembering takes us outside the confines of domesticity and an individual existence and forces us to reassemble, filtered through an individual story, a whole social world and, beyond it, a whole culture. Bridging the gap between the 1920s and the dawn of a new century, Amantea tells not only the story of two individuals almost lost to history but also the multiplicity of stories through which the account of their lives will necessarily be refracted. In the simplest of terms, the book reconstructs the lives of two Italian immigrants, Filumena Lassandro, née Costanzo, and Emilio Picariello.* In some ways, Filumena, or Florence, as she was better known, and "Emperor Pic" cover the spectrum of the immigrant experience. At one end, we have a man who, at first glance, seems to embody the American (and Canadian) dream. After arriving in Fernie, British Columbia, in 1911 by way of Toronto, Picariello went on to become a successful businessman (he earned his nickname reselling, in what must surely be one of the first recycling schemes in the world, used bottles to the Alberta government, thus becoming the de facto "Bottle King" of the province) and local politician, as well as the patriarch of a large family in which, as in the monarchy governing the country, his eldest son, Stefano (or Steve), was destined to replace him as the head of his empire. At the other end, we find the dark side of that same dream, the all-too-common story of a poor and semi-literate immigrant girl uprooted from her native Calabria at the age of six, then handed over in marriage at fourteen to a man ten years her senior to live a life of submissiveness, loneliness, and sacrifice. For both the dream would end in tragedy. After Alberta went dry in 1916, Picariello switched his business from bottles to their content, first manufacturing the low-alcohol beer permitted by the new prohibitionist legislation and then smuggling alcohol across the American border. Filumena entered his orbit when her husband, Carlo, started working for him, and she may have had (the rumours were never confirmed) an affair with Steve Picariello, who on 21 September 1922 was wounded by Stephen Lawson, an officer of the Alberta Provincial Police, and arrested.

* Many names that appear in the book may not be accurate or spelled correctly in Italian. Names and spellings were often the interpretations of immigration officials. These versions were perpetuated through usage and the often limited literacy of the immigrants themselves. At the same time names were further distorted by newspapers and bureaucracies which commonly recorded even these versions incorrectly.

This is where the official records fail us: later that day Emilio and Filumena turned up at the APP headquarters to discuss the situation with Lawson, there was a struggle, and the officer was shot dead. How and why the altercation began and who in fact fired the shot has never been satisfactorily explained. In the end, Emilio and Filumena were tried for murder and sentenced to death by hanging. Filumena was the last woman to be executed in Alberta.

It is at this point that history, to which this story is nothing more than a footnote, and personal memory connect, since Amantea first heard of Emilio and Filumena, now part of the lore of the western Canadian Italian community, from her own father, who was born and grew up in Fernie. Thus the years of archival work that resulted in this volume are, at least initially, a response to the desire to understand a very specific and, indeed, local story that is, however, also emblematic of the contradictions of the Canadian immigrant experience. By what tortuous ways did a young Italian woman come to hang on the gallows in Alberta? As a result of what cultural and social prejudices was she inflicted with the ultimate punishment, when genteel women of English descent found guilty of comparable crimes were, by virtue of their gender, granted clemency as a matter of course and had their sentence commuted to life in prison? And, perhaps most importantly for an artist, how does one tell this story without falling into melodrama? As in *Requiescat* but on the larger canvas of history, the act of remembrance is thus endowed with the ethical responsibility of rescuing from oblivion, reconstructing, and giving meaning to two severed lives.

The book *The King v. Picariello and Lassandro* began as an art installation for the Dunlop Art Gallery in the Regina Public Library, where it was first shown in 2002. The principle governing the fourteen large-size panels, re-edited for a remarkable short film and the present volume, is that of collage, with its startling juxtapositions of disparate elements, from historical documents to personal photographs and images from popular culture. The opening pages reconstruct in all its fullness a world now gone. From the establishing shot of early-twentieth-century Fernie to the list of alien immigrants, in which individual lives are reduced to entries in a bureaucratic questionnaire; from the gaping maw of a mine entrance to the vertical section of a miner's house, in which the threadbare and forlorn furniture, like the armchair and television set in *and sorrow come near us no more*, are witness to the vanished existence of its owners; the images forcefully assert the importance of understanding the historical reality in which the events told in the book took place. Filumena's and Emilio's story cannot be properly comprehended without being placed in the context of the ethnic and class tensions permeating Canadian society at the beginning of the century – tensions explored in the chapter "Labour and Race," which includes, among many striking images and documents (a miners' demonstration under the banner "Karl Marx Park," the prison-like square building of an internment camp), a letter that stands out for the brutal honesty of its system of ethnic taxonomy: "These people," writes a B.C. Land Commissioner regarding a group of Tuscan immigrants, "are not the usual Dago class, but the better class of Italian peasantry."

At the same time, Amantea details the everyday reality of the men and women dislocated by emigration. In a beautiful montage in the chapter titled "Filumena," the quotidian rituals revolving around food become real through the introduction of a series of what we might call *objets trouvés* – the recipe for a cake known as *pizzachiusa*, two photographs of Amantea's own family – shards of reality that suddenly make a whole cultural world arise in all its richness. The evocative power of these images derives precisely from the fact that they straddle that divide between public and private which we have had occasion to mention before, as they are simultaneously representative of a milieu and the traces of particular, individual lives and experiences. In fact, without a doubt one of the most significant elements of Amantea's art is her attention to detail, as a result of which her work, like documentary, has a texture, density, and breadth of reference that exceeds its narrative form. Consider, for instance, the image of the Asian cowboy in "Labour and Race." The subject has the gravity of an equestrian monument, yet at the same time he is immediately recognizable, because of his clothes and the harness of his horse, rendered in minute detail, as an inhabitant of the milieu so lovingly portrayed in the book.

The author is not only interested in reconstructing the sociopolitical world of western Canada circa 1920, however. The story of Filumena and Emilio is also the stuff of drama, and Amantea solves, with a brilliant move, the problem of how one can write about bootlegging and murder without immediately setting in motion the intertextual competence of any reader, for whom such things are inevitably linked with their representation in Hollywood cinema. Indeed, the more dramatic and adventurous parts of the story, those regarding Steve's chase and wounding and the murder of the APP officer, are filtered through our cultural imagination, reinterpreted through the great tradition of noir and pulp cinema, which was in its turn inspired by real-life crime. We half recognize the images – Faye Dunaway from *Bonnie and Clyde*, Humphrey Bogart from *High Sierra*, Al Pacino from *Heat* – given coherence by the artist's tracing, which, as Nancy Tousley has written in an article on the 2002 exhibition, "unifies the differences and contradictions without suppressing them" (*Canadian Art*, Spring 2003, p. 64). Through this technique, Amantea brings together and contaminates in this sequence, perhaps the most complex of the book, private story, public history, and cultural imagination. For a moment, Filumena and Emilio become characters of legendary proportions, almost archetypal (the femme fatale, the godfather). But as their story continues beyond the point when Hollywood films usually end and it details the trial and retribution of the protagonists, reality reasserts itself, and we are again confronted with two immigrants caught in the wheels of a machine well beyond their control. The hanging bodies have none of the glamour of noir cinema; they look rather like empty sacks, forgotten objects like the chair with which we began our discussion, mute signs of a vanished existence. The article from *La Tribuna Canadiana*, which closes the book with a denunciation of the racist double standard of Filumena's death sentence, provides a fitting social commentary on the events. But among the documents of the time assembled in the final chapters, the one that stays with the reader is certainly Emilio's last letter to his wife, with its disarming simplicity and dignity in the face of death ("I want you to know that I do not owe any body"). In the final lines, a postscript to his own life, Emilio scribbles down his brother's and his mother's address back in Italy, entrusting himself to their memory as he prepares to exit from the stage of history.

LUCA SOMIGLI is Associate Professor of Italian Studies at the University of Toronto.

Fernie ca. 1908

AT THE BEGINNING OF THE TWENTIETH CENTURY MANY IMMIGRANTS TRAVELED TO FERNIE TO FIND WORK IN THE COALMINES. THE TOWN WAS NAMED AFTER WILLIAM FERNIE, WHO LEFT ENGLAND IN 1853 AND EVENTUALLY WENT TO THE INTERIOR OF BRITISH COLUMBIA IN THE LATE 1880S. HE TOOK LAND, RICH IN COAL DEPOSITS, FROM THE INDIGENOUS PEOPLE BY MEANS

OF DECEPTION. THE IMMIGRANTS WHO COULD SPEAK ENGLISH AND WERE BRITISH SUBJECTS BECAME THE FOREMEN IN THE MINES, OWNED THE HOTELS AND BUSINESSES. THE MAJORITY OF THE WORKERS WERE NOT LITERATE — THEY WERE FOR THE MOST PART UKRAINIANS, ITALIANS, SLAVS AND CHINESE.

NAVIGAZIONE GENERALE ITALIANA
Societa Rvinito
FLORIO- BUBATTINO

Capitale Stipiaro L.60,000,000 - Enesso L.33,000,000

LIST OF ALIEN IMMIGRANT

Required by the regulations of the secretary of the treasu
to the Commissioner of Immigration by the

SS. CITTA di Milano sailing from Napoli, 10 December

1	2	3	4	5	6	7		8	9	10	11	12
No. on List	Name in Full	Age	Sex	Marry or Single	Calling	Able to Read	Able to Write	Nationality	Last Residence	Seaport for Landing in the United States	Final Destination in the United States (state, city or town)	Whether having a ticket to such a final destination
1	Volpicelli, Guido	29	M	M	peasant	no	no	Italian	Pisano	New York	New York	yes
2	Pace, Salvatore	27	M	M	peasant	no	no	Italian	Sagurgola	New York	New York	yes
3	Parasiderio, Giuseppe	44	M	M	peasant	no	no	Italian	Cinquefrondi	New York	Boston, Mas	no
4	Santopinto, Riccardo	28	M	M	labourer	yes	yes	Italian	Antrodoco	New York	Calgary, Alberta	yes
5	Santopinto, Nicola	23	M	M	labourer	yes	yes	Italian	Antrodoco	New York	"	yes
6	Marasco, Maria	26	F	M	wife	no	no	Italian	Rochester	New York	New York	yes
7	" , Teresina	6	F	S	child	no	no	Italian	"	"	"	"
8	" , Rosina	9m	F	S	child	no	no	Italian	"	"	"	-
9	Cioni, Gisa	19y	F	S	housewife	yes	yes	Italian	Antrodoco	New York	Calgary, Alberta	n
10	Castrucci, Angela	22	F	S				Italy	Antrodoco	New York	Calgary, Canada	yes
11	Cuffa, Agata	32	F	M				Italian	Antrodoco	New York	"	yes
12	Aquilini, Barbara	8m	F	S	child	no	no	Italian	Antrodoco	New York	"	"
13	Aquilini, Cesarina	24	F	S	child	no	no	Italian	Antrodoco	New York	"	"

E COMMISSIONER OF IMMIGRATION

ited States, under Act of Congress approved March 3, 1893, to be delivered
officer of any vessel having such passengers on board upon arrival at a port in the United States

ing at Port of New York, December 26, 1902

14	15	16	17	18	19	20	21
Whether in possession of money. If so whether more than $30 and how much if $30 or less	Whether ever before in the United States, and if so where and when	Whether going to join a relative and if so, what relative, their name and address	Ever in Prison or Almshouse or supported by charity. If yes state which	Whether a Polygamist	Whether under contract express or implied to labour in the United States	Condition of health mental and physical	Deformed or Crippl[ed] Nature, length of time, cau[se]
$10	no	nobody	no	no	no	good	no
$13	no	nobody	no	no	no	good	no
$12	no	cousin Penose, M 192 North St, Boston	no	no	no	good	no
$15	no	nobody	no	no	no	good	no
$12	no	nobody	no	no	no	good	no
$16	yes	sister Rosa Manos Rochester	no	no	no	good	no
"	"	"	"	"	"	"	"
"	"	"	"	"	"	"	"
$25	no	husband 434 E. 14 NYK	no	no	no	good	no
$22	no	bride going Pietro Cuffo	no	no	no	good	no
$35	no	husband	no	no	no	good	no
"	"	father Aquilen Antonio	no	no	no	good	no
"	"	father M. Mutal	no	no	no	good	no

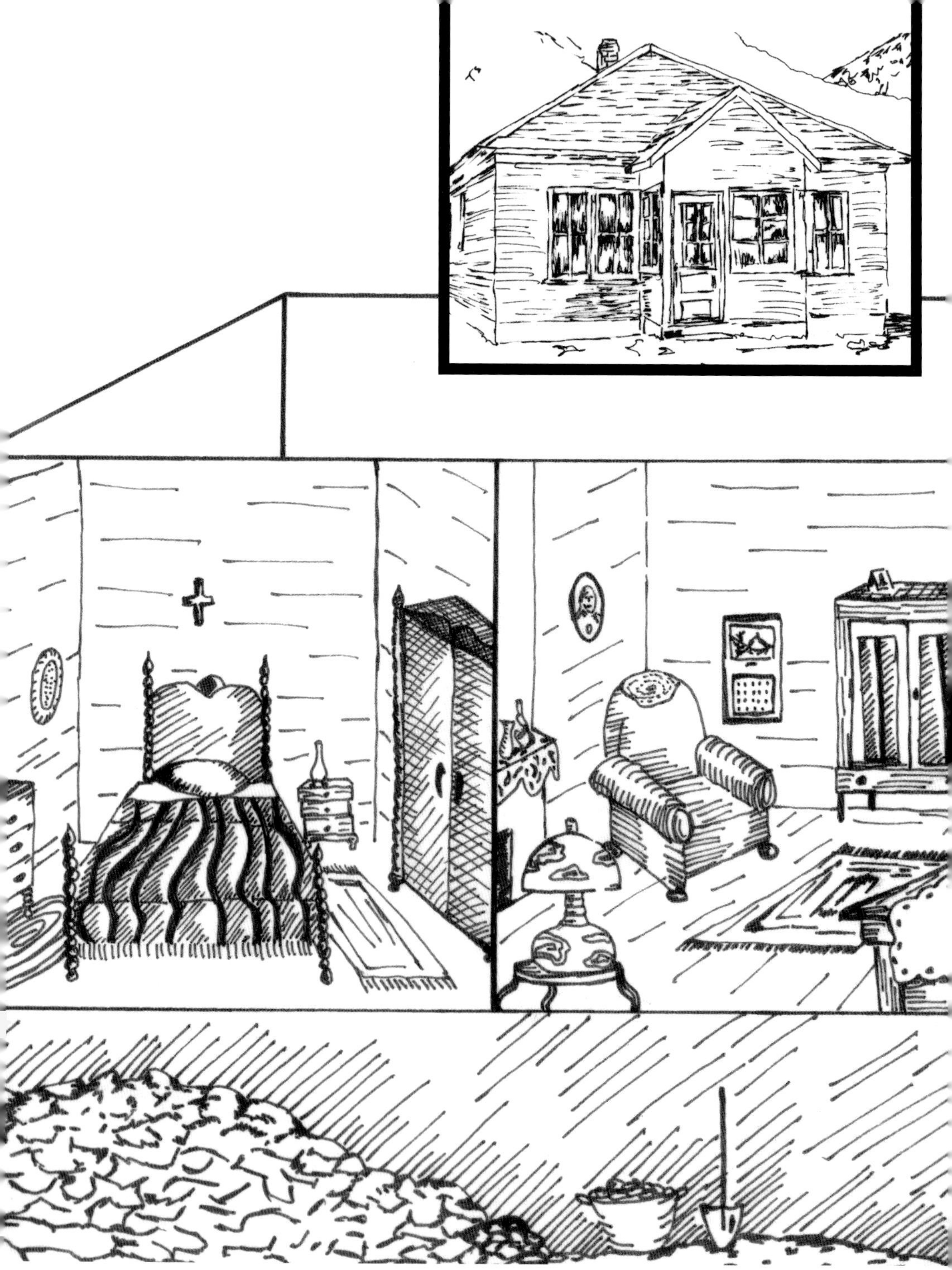

MINER'S HOUSE

FERNIE was one of a number of mining towns located in the British Columbia – Alberta border area that spans the Elk Valley and Crowsnest Pass. Ethnic groups were segregated

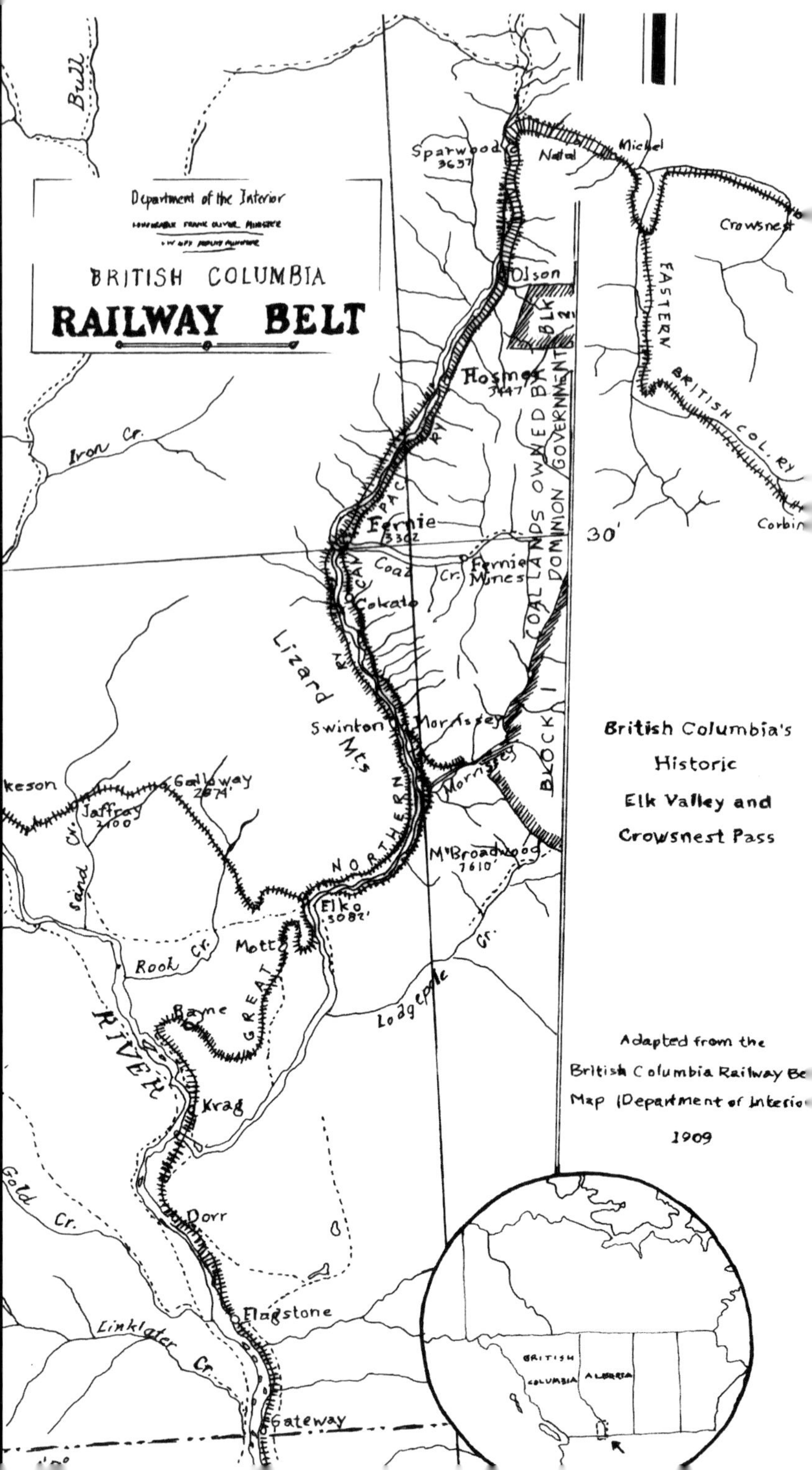

British Columbia's Historic Elk Valley and Crowsnest Pass

Adapted from the British Columbia Railway Belt Map (Department of Interior) 1909

As towns developed these groups began to establish themselves — marriages were arranged with young girls via the "old country" or from the community itself.

The Mines

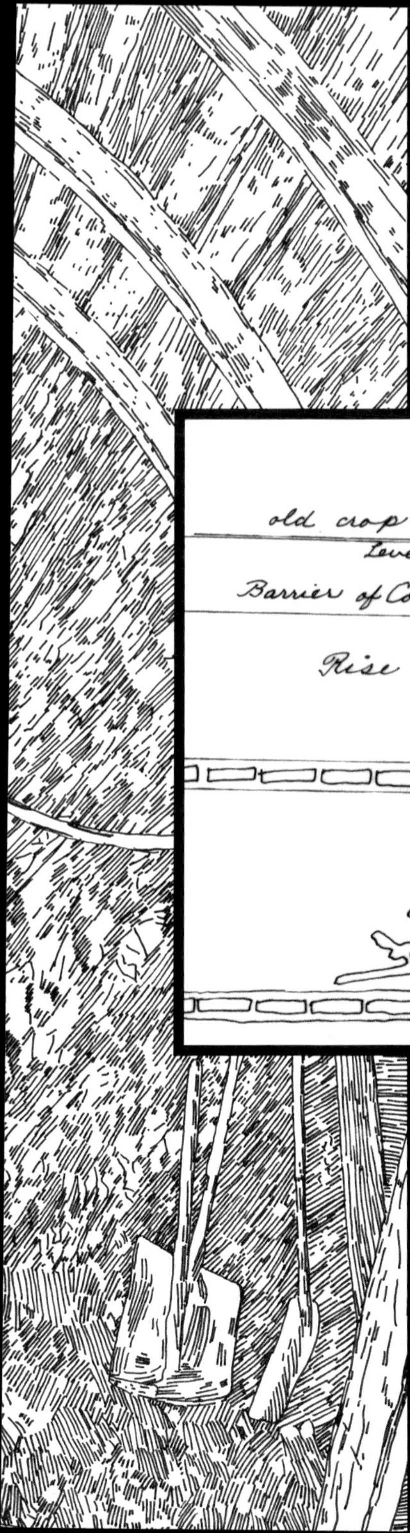

INTERIOR OF MINE

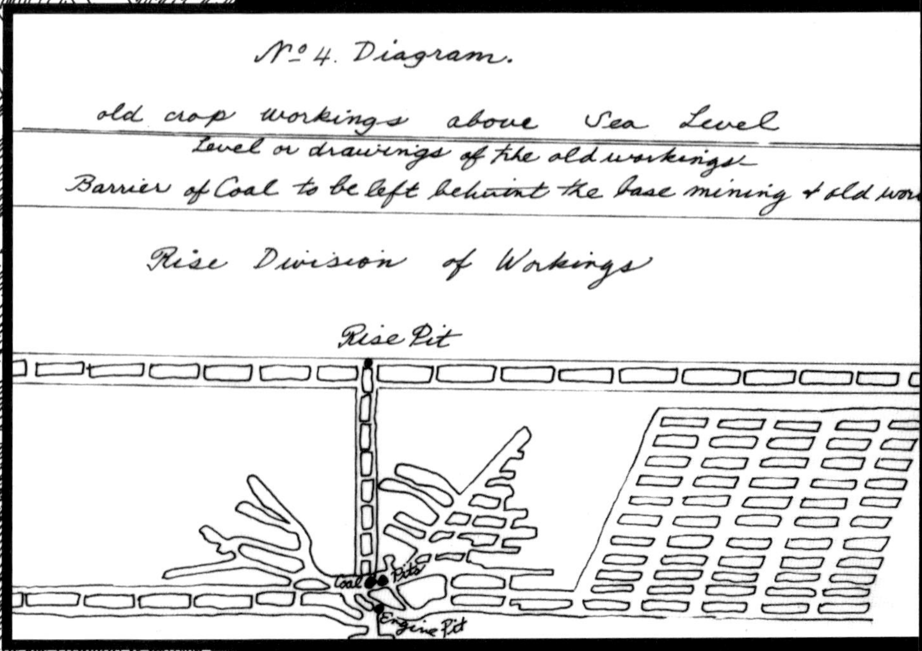

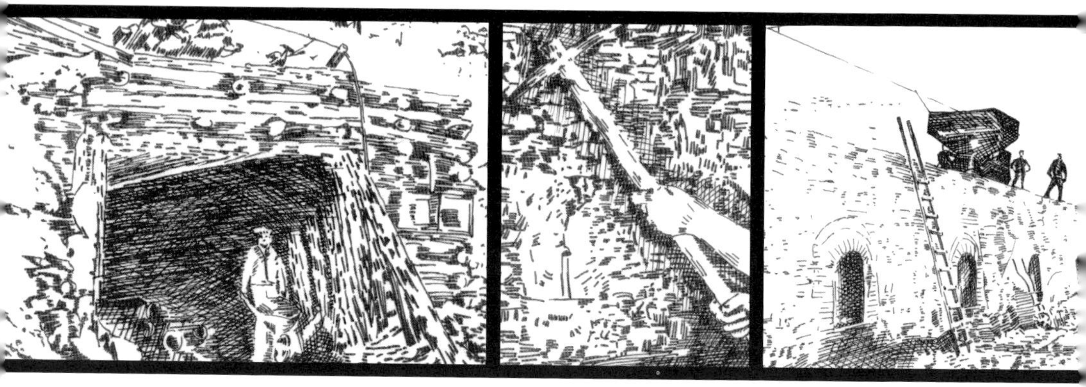

WORK AT THE COKE OVENS was especially strenuous. One man would be responsible for six ovens. Men of sturdy physique were required — preferably of Slavic origin. Normally each day one man would pull five or six tons of radiating hot coke with a sixty-pound shovel. Wages were $1 or less for each oven as it was emptied of coke. Coke ovens were located close to railway tracks and in town. They burned twenty-four hours a day.

Men and boys worked underground. They dug coal by hand with minimal and inadequate equipment. Shifts were ten hours a day, six days a week. At times miners walked two hours underground — time not paid — to begin work.

THE GREATEST DANGER WORKING IN THE MINES WAS FROM POISONOUS GAS RELEASED BY DIGGING OR FROM THE LARGE QUANTITIES OF DUST THAT LINGERED IN THE AIR IGNITING AND CAUSING AN EXPLOSION. FROM 1879 TO 1917, 862 MINERS DIED IN ACCIDENTS IN BRITISH COLUMBIA AND ALBERTA.

ETHNIC TENSIONS AND CLASS CONFLICTS WERE EXACERBATED BY A HIERARCHICAL LABOUR STRUCTURE, CONSTANTLY CHANGING MARKET CONDITIONS, LACK OF PLANNING BY THE FEDERAL GOVERNMENT AND GREEDY COAL COMPANIES THAT WERE ESTABLISHED AT THIS TIME.

Filumena

IN 1906 FILUMENA COSTANZO IMMIGRATED TO FERNIE FROM COSENZA, A TOWN IN THE CALABRIA REGION OF SOUTHERN ITALY. SHE WAS SIX YEARS OLD. HER FATHER VINCENZO WAS FIRST EMPLOYED ON THE RAILWAY AND HE LATER WORKED IN THE COALMINES.

FILUMENA WAS ONE OF THREE CHILDREN. SHE GREW UP WITH A STRONG UNDERSTANDING OF THE VALUE OF HARD WORK. ENTIRE FAMILIES OF LABOURERS WORKED. GIRLS MOST OFTEN HELPED OUT AT HOME. BOYS WORKED IN THE MINES, SHINED SHOES OR DID ODD JOBS.

SCHOOL WAS LIMITED TO THE EARLY GRADES WHERE CHILDREN LEARNED TO READ AND WRITE IN ENGLISH. THEY PERFORMED IMPORTANT TASKS FOR THEIR PARENTS — WRITING LETTERS TO FAMILY IN ITALY, TRANSLATING INFORMATION AND COMMUNICATING WITH NON-ITALIANS.

PIZZACHIUSA

6 cups flour

6 teaspoons baking powder

4 eggs (if small use six beaten)

1 1/4 cups milk

1 cup lard

2/3 cup butter

Sift together flour and baking powder. Warm milk and add to it the shortening and butter, melt and then let cool. Make a well in the centre of flour, to it add milk, butter and beaten eggs. Mix well, no need to knead, let rest for at least one hour.

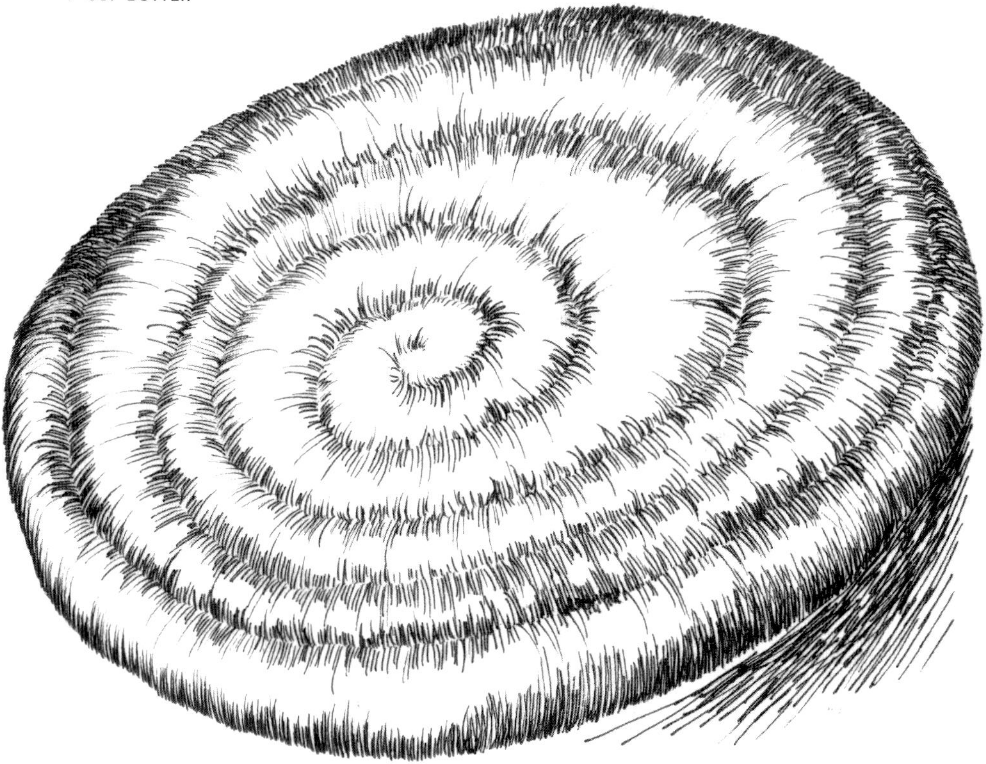

FILLING

1 pound raisins sprinkled with cinnamon

walnuts

almonds, slightly toasted

honey

olive oil

cinnamon

powdered cloves

1/2 pound almonds with skin and chopped

1/2 pound walnuts, chopped

Roll out a sheet of dough spread with oil then sugar and cinnamon. Cover with raisins and nuts, form into a roll and spread with liquid honey. Roll into a coil and cover with oil, sugar and cinnamon. Roll out a smaller sheet of dough, cover with oil, sugar and cinnamon. Place coil on this smaller sheet and bring dough up around the coil. Use wooden sticks to hold dough in place. Bake in a 350° oven for about 35 minutes or until nice and golden. When removed from oven and still warm, pour oil and honey into circles of dough. Set cake to cool for at least one day.

FOOD WAS AN IMPORTANT REMINDER OF HOME. GIRLS LEARNED TO MAKE TRADITIONAL FAVOURITES SUCH AS PIZZACHIUSA, A CHRISTMAS CAKE, AND PEOPLE OFTEN WENT TO GREAT LENGTHS TO GROW VEGETABLES AND FIND INGREDIENTS FOR FAMILIAR FOODS. GARDENS WITH FAVA BEANS AND TOMATOES WERE CULTIVATED IN THE DITCHES ALONG THE ROADS. MUSHROOMS WERE PICKED IN THE MOUNTAINS. DURING THE SUMMER, PICNICS PROVIDED THE MAJOR FORM OF CELEBRATION AND COMMUNITY GATHERINGS.

THE CATHOLIC CHURCH LOOMED LARGE IN THE SMALL TOWNS THROUGHOUT THE PASS. LOCAL COMMUNITIES STRUGGLED TO BUILD CHURCHES AND TO ESTABLISH LODGES FOR MEN AND SOCIAL CLUBS FOR WOMEN.

WHEN FILUMENA WAS FOURTEEN YEARS OLD, CARLO SANFIDELE, A MAN TEN YEARS HER SENIOR, BECAME INTERESTED IN FILUMENA AND BEGAN DISCUSSING MARRIAGE WITH HER FATHER. CUSTOM, POVERTY, XENOPHOBIA AND LARGE FAMILIES OFTEN NECESSITATED THAT THE OLDEST GIRLS IN THE FAMILY WERE LITERALLY TREATED AS CHATTEL. IT WAS NOT UNCOMMON FOR A YOUNG GIRL TO BE WON OR LOST IN A CARD GAME.

MARRIAGE WAS A LONELY PROSPECT FOR FILUMENA. THIS INTENSIFIED WHEN CARLO DECIDED THAT THEY WOULD RELOCATE TO NORTHERN PENNSYLVANIA.

Emperor Pic

EMILIO PICARIELLO was born in 1875 and emigrated from southern Italy at the turn of the twentieth century. He first went to the United States and then to Toronto where he met and married Marionina Marucci, a member of the Italian immigrant community.

In 1911 the Picariello family moved to Fernie. There he was involved in various business ventures. He operated a confectionery and cigar business and built a successful ice cream company. In 1914 he became the sales representative for a legal liquor business and sold alcohol to establishments throughout the Pass.

Emilio Picariello was ambitious and charming — a large and generous man. His intelligence manifested itself in understanding how to thrive in difficult times. Throughout his life he gave to the community. During strikes, he distributed food to the miners' families and where possible, assisted those in need. In January 1921 Emilio Picariello was elected to the Blairmore town council.

In 1916 Emilio began to collect used bottles in his spare time — soon he had collected thousands and began to resell them. One of his largest clients was the Alberta government. It was through this activity that he became known as Emperor Pic — "the bottle king."

Emilio and Marionina had seven children — Stefano, Angelina, Carmine, Louis, Charles, Albert and Florence. Stefano (Steve), the eldest son, was a young teenager when Prohibition came to Alberta. In Italian families eldest sons were cherished and great expectations were placed upon them. Steve was brought into the business. One of his duties was to drive shipments of alcohol into British Columbia and Montana.

IN 1918 EMILIO PURCHASED THE ALBERTA HOTEL AND MOVED TO BLAIRMORE, ALBERTA. THE HOTEL WAS TYPICAL OF THE TIME. THERE WAS A BAR AND A FEW BUSINESSES ON THE MAIN FLOOR. ROOMS UPSTAIRS WERE RENTED. THIS WAS ALSO WHERE THE FAMILY LIVED. THE BACK OF THE HOTEL HAD A STEEP SLOPE AND CARS COULD DRIVE INTO A LOADING DOCK THAT WAS PRIVATE AND PARTLY HIDDEN.

The lives of men and women were separate. There was a strong male culture and many single men came to work in the Pass. Drinking was one of their few forms of entertainment and the dominant cultural custom in this era. When Alberta voted to go dry in 1916 a large majority in the Pass voted to stay wet.

During Prohibition Emilio sold "temperance" beer, which contained 2½% alcohol. During the first years of Prohibition it was legal to make and import alcohol but not to drink it. Many people were accustomed to making their own alcohol and Emilio thrived on selling stronger brew. Also, he was in a prime location — close to the border of British Columbia and Montana and in an area where mountain roads made it difficult to track movement. The area south of Fernie, known as Tobacco Plains, provided an opening in the mountains where powerful McLaughlin cars (known as Whiskey Sixes) could drive cross country and into the United States.

One of Emperor Pic's closest associates was Carlo Sanfidele, who returned in 1917 from living in Pennsylvania. In keeping with a common practice among immigrants, he and Filumena anglicized their names and at this time became known as Charles and Florence Lassandro.

Labour and Racism

July 18th, 1904

J.S. Dennis Esq.,
B.C. Land Commissioner
Calgary, Alta.

Dear Sir,

Mr. George H. Ham has written me that Dr. Bryce, Chief Medical Officer of the Department of the Interior, Ottawa, tells him that enquiries are being made by a number of the better class of people of Tuscany and thereabouts regarding lands in Canada. These people Mr. Ham understands are not the usual Dago class, but the better class of Italian peasantry.

I do not think the climate of Manitoba, or the Territories would suit these people. British Columbia would be better in that respect.

Will you kindly write Dr. Bryce and give him your ideas as to the best location. I suppose the difficulty would be in finding suitable lands at a reasonable price. Mr. Ham may possibly have already communicated with you on this subject.

Yours truly,

F.T. Griffin
Land Commissioner

British Columbia Archives, Victoria, British Columbia Attorney general Fonds

Re: Report on the oriental situation in British Columbia. (1922)
Report by the General Ministerial Association of Vancouver regarding the status of Chinese, Japanese and Hindu [also used to denote Sikhs] in the province, as well as suggestions on dealing with the "problem" of their presence.

Re: A Chinese petition. (1891)
Petition from Chinese citizens of Kootney in original Chinese and English translation, regarding ill treatment suffered at the hands of the local Justice of the Peace.

Re: Italians going hungry in Fort Steele. (1898)
Correspondence from local Government officials regarding large number of unemployed Italian railway workers seeking government relief at Fort Steele.

Re: Chinese man murdered by boy. (1900)
An account of the murder of a Chinese resident of Rossland, B.C. and the suspicion being placed on a nine year-old boy of the town.

Re: Boy confesses to shooting Chinese man. (1900)
Regarding development in the case when suspect confesses to murder under examination of the Pinkerton agency.

Re: Boy kills Chinese man. (1900)
Further development in the case where additional witnesses come forward to tell that suspect confessed the murder to them and that it was racially motivated.

Re: Fernie Mine Trouble. (1902)
Account of local constable regarding labour unrest in Fernie, B.C. including opinion on the temperaments of the races involved.

Re: Mob opposes coming of Oriental employees. (1905)
Report of police activity to protect Oriental workers hired by a shingle plant in Salmo from a white mob meaning to oppose them.

Re: F.J. Lascelles under arrest pending investigation of murder. (1901)
British ex-patriot under arrest after murdering his Chinese manservant.

Re: Lascelles murder of Chinese manservant. (1901)
Telegraph to Attorney General regarding Lascelles' confinement as insane.

Re: Report from the Provincial Asylum for the Insane. (1901)
Report from superintendent of the Provincial Asylum regarding Lascelles' sanity.

Re: Removal of Lascelles to England. (1901)
Attempt by Lascelles' family lawyers to free him from the Insane Asylum and bring him to England.

Re: Correspondence of the Provincial Asylum for the Insane to Attorney General.
Reversal of previous recommendation by Asylum superintendent to hand Lascelles over to his relatives' care.

Re: F. Lascelles acquitted of murder. (1901)
Acquittal of Lascelles on count of murder due to his insanity.

Re: Lascelles released to his relatives. (1901)
Lascelles freed from asylum and handed over to relatives to his return to England. [Lascelles would go on to live comfortably on his family's estate, fully acquitted of the murder of his servant. A small time later, however, Lascelles would take his own life with a self-inflicted gunshot wound.]

Re: Strike in Michel, B.C. (1906)
Report by local constable regarding damage caused by striking workers, including theories of involvement by local ethnic groups.

Re: Conviction of members of a Black Hand, Fernie, B.C. (1908)
List of charges and documentation of the conviction of members of a criminal conspiracy going by the name "Black Hand" in Fernie, B.C.

NTERNMENT CAMP,
1ORRISSEY — 1915

Re: Black Hand trouble at Fernie, B.C. (1909)
Complaints from Italian citizens regarding threats being made against their lives due to their work in convicting Black Hand members in Fernie.

Re: Black Hand troubles in Revelstoke. (1909)
Includes correspondence regarding the prosecution of three individuals in Revelstoke who passed themselves off as the Black Hand. Also includes accounts of larger public reaction and discrimination against all Italian citizens.

Re: Chinamen cannot pre-empt. (1910)
Correspondence regarding the fact that Chinese citizens are forbidden by government's Land Act from obtaining any Crown land.

<u>**National Archives of Canada, Ottawa, Ontario**</u>

Re: Lt. Governor reports on leprosy among Chinese & establishment of lazaretto. (1892)
Correspondence between B.C. representatives and Secretary of State regarding state of Chinese population in B.C. and implications for foreign relations.

Re: Act of B.C. legislature on use of Chinese labour for CPR construction. (1884)
Legislative measure regarding imitations on contractors' preferred use of Chinese labour for CPR work.

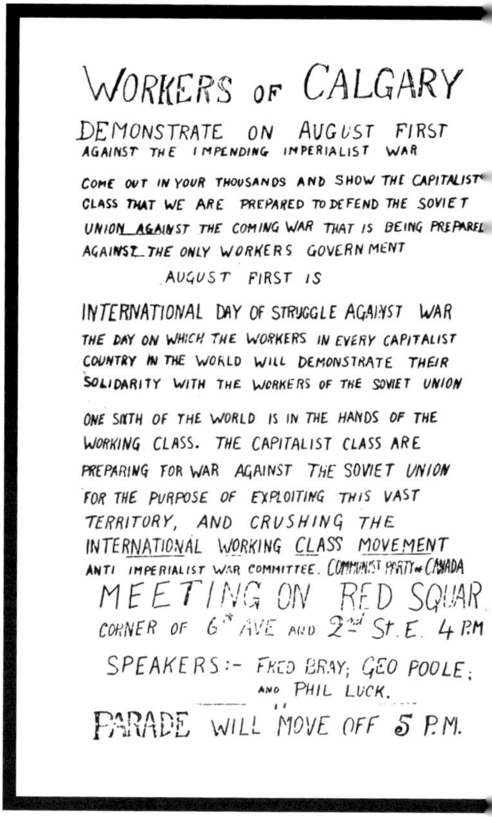

WORKERS OF CALGARY
DEMONSTRATE ON AUGUST FIRST
AGAINST THE IMPENDING IMPERIALIST WAR
COME OUT IN YOUR THOUSANDS AND SHOW THE CAPITALIST CLASS THAT WE ARE PREPARED TO DEFEND THE SOVIET UNION AGAINST THE COMING WAR THAT IS BEING PREPARED AGAINST THE ONLY WORKERS GOVERNMENT
AUGUST FIRST IS
INTERNATIONAL DAY OF STRUGGLE AGAINST WAR
THE DAY ON WHICH THE WORKERS IN EVERY CAPITALIST COUNTRY IN THE WORLD WILL DEMONSTRATE THEIR SOLIDARITY WITH THE WORKERS OF THE SOVIET UNION
ONE SIXTH OF THE WORLD IS IN THE HANDS OF THE WORKING CLASS. THE CAPITALIST CLASS ARE PREPARING FOR WAR AGAINST THE SOVIET UNION FOR THE PURPOSE OF EXPLOITING THIS VAST TERRITORY, AND CRUSHING THE INTERNATIONAL WORKING CLASS MOVEMENT
ANTI IMPERIALIST WAR COMMITTEE. COMMUNIST PARTY of CANADA
MEETING ON RED SQUAR
CORNER OF 6th AVE AND 2nd St. E. 4 P.M
SPEAKERS:- FRED BRAY; GEO POOLE; AND PHIL LUCK.
PARADE WILL MOVE OFF 5 P.M.

Re: Report on utilizing white over Chinese labour in B.C. (1882)
Situations report to federal department regarding the situation regarding Chinese labour being used for agricultural work in B.C.

Re: Constitution of the Italian Immigration Aid Society of Canada. (1904)
Royal Commission report and supporting documents regarding the large influx of Italian people into Canada via Montreal.

<u>**Royal Commission to Investigate Chinese and Japanese Immigration into British Columbia, 1900-1902.**</u>

Re: Chinese Immigration:
Putting Up Bars Against Chinese." and " An Act to Restrict Chinese Immigration."

Re: Chinese Immigration (report by W.L.M. King); "An Act to amend the Chinese Immigration Act." and "Chinese Immigration Act, 1910."

Re: U.S. Treaty, Laws and Regulations Concerning the Admission of Chinese, 1911.
Reports and supporting documents regarding the Royal Commission on Oriental Immigration held in 1908. Includes a very interesting translation of Chinese circular sent to China describing the bad conditions and injustices Chinese people face in Canada.

Re: Report of the Crowsnest Pass Railway Commission
Crowsnest Pass Railway Commission, Working papers & correspondence. Reports, transcripts and working papers of a commission founded to look into the poor working and living conditions on the construction of the Crowsnest Railway. Commission was prompted by reports of unhealthy conditions and deaths arising during this project.

<u>Canadian Pacific Railway Fonds</u>

Re: Correspondence regarding Italian settlement.
Various letters between CPR officials, B.C. Government officials and Italian representatives regarding proposed settlement of Italian farmers in the fruit growing regions of British Columbia.

Re: Letter regarding Chinese immigration. (1907)
Letter from CPR staff member to president regarding Chinese people immigrating from Hong Kong and whether status as British citizens makes them exempt from paying the head tax.

<u>CPR Records Collection</u>

Re: Letter Mehar Sing to CPR Superintendent, Revelstoke. (1909)
Letter regarding the mistreatment of East Indian workers on CPR work and bosses' favouritism toward new Italian labourers.

<u>Revelstoke City Record Collection</u>

Re: Request from City Council to CPR regarding land sales. (1901)
Request from Revelstoke City Council on behalf of the city residents to not sell land in areas of Revelstoke to Chinese people.

Re: Destitution among Chinese CPR workers. (1886)

Re: Act to be passed placing special taxes on Chinese (1880)

Florence and Charles

FLORENCE AND CHARLES LIVED IN ROOMS ON THE SECOND FLOOR OF THE ALBERTA HOTEL. WHILE CHARLES WORKED FOR EMILIO, FLORENCE HELPED WITH HOUSEKEEPING AND THE CARE OF EMILIO AND MARIONINA'S CHILDREN. FLORENCE AND CHARLES DID NOT HAVE CHILDREN OF THEIR OWN AND SHE VALUED BEING PART OF THIS LARGE EXTENDED FAMILY.

ONE OF FLORENCE'S OTHER DUTIES WAS TO ASSIST IN THE TRANSPORTATION OF ILLEGAL ALCOHOL. SHE WAS CLOSE IN AGE TO STEVE AND THEY FREQUENTLY MADE TRIPS TOGETHER INTO THE MOUNTAINS — AT TIMES SHE WOULD DRIVE THE CAR AS THEY TRAVELED TO FERNIE TO PICK UP A LOAD OF ILLEGAL ALCOHOL AND RETURN TO HIDE THE WHISKEY IN CELLARS BENEATH THE HOTEL. AT TIMES, THEY WOULD NOT TRANSPORT THE ALCOHOL BUT INSTEAD ACTED AS DECOYS FOR THE POLICE. THEY WOULD STOP FOR LONG AFTERNOON PICNICS IN THE MOUNTAINS. OCCASIONALLY, EVEN FLORENCE'S NIECE WOULD ACCOMPANY THEM ON THESE EXCURSIONS. EMILIO (RIGHTLY) THOUGHT IF A WOMAN WAS IN THE CAR THE POLICE WOULD NOT OPEN FIRE IN PURSUIT OF A SUSPICIOUS VEHICLE.

FLORENCE WAS NOT FULFILLED IN HER MARRIAGE TO CHARLES. SHE FOUND COMPANIONSHIP IN HER RELATIONSHIP WITH STEVE. SHE WAS WELL CARED FOR AND PROTECTED BY EMILIO — SHE GAVE HER TRUST TO BOTH OF THEM.

Prohibition

CAN THE BAR-TENDERS DRAW THE COLOR LINE IN PROVINCE OF ALTA.

Edmonton, April 9.—"Have Edmonton bartenders the right to draw the color line?" That is the question which has been raised by a couple of dark skinned citizens who visited the license department this morning to lay a complaint before the chief license inspector. "Togged out" in the most fashionable of American clothes, almost dandified in their get up and in their bearing, the negroes invaded the department to find out whether the act-ion of the bartenders of two local hotels in refusing to serve them with lrinks was "according to the law" or no. Chief Inspector Foster was away und the negroes were unable to obtain the satisfaction for which they sought.

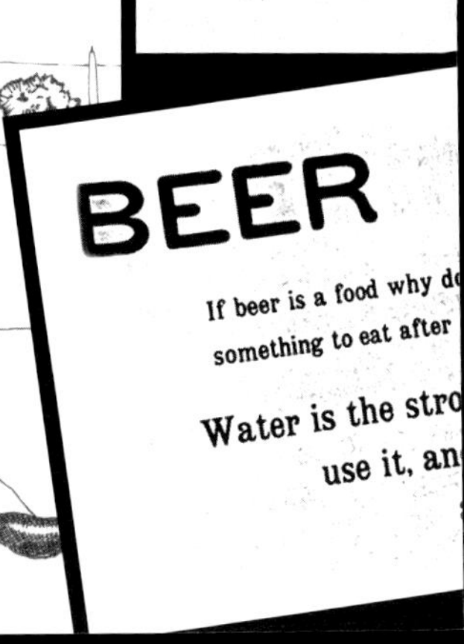

ANTED! By LIQUOR TRAFFIC

Thousand New Canadian Fathers and Sons

Thousand New Canadian Men and Boys

TO TAKE THE PLACE OF

Ten Thousand Drunkards Dead!

OLISH THE BAR

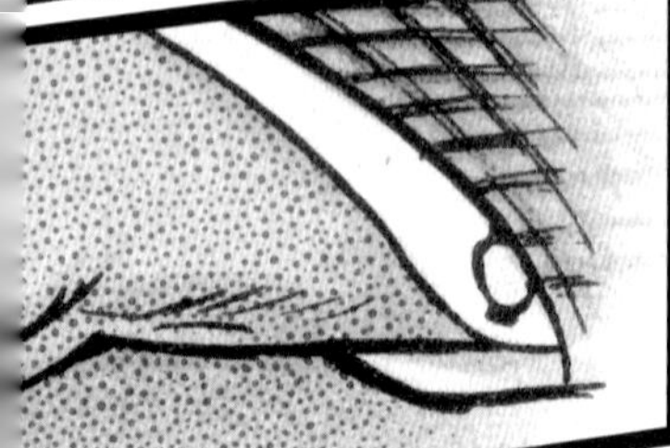

MY

E AND

ST HERE

PROVINCE OF ALBERTA

LIQUOR PRESCRIPTION

No. 37190

DATE..........................1922

ONLY VALID FOR AUGUST, 1922

REQUIRED for Mr.......................................

Address.......................................

....

....

....

....

Signature and Address of Physician.

RECEIVED from.......................................

Medicine as above prescribed.

BOOK 633 ....

....

Signature and Address of Person Receiving Liquor.

FOOD

ee a man begging for

n a three days' drunk.

k; lions and horses

never drank

else.

THE

LIQUOR TRAFFIC

MUST GO

THE REVENUE IS SMALL COMPARED WITH THE COST

IT CAUSES

Poverty, Misery and Crime

THE REMEDY

NATIONAL CONSTITUTIONAL PROHIBITION

ALCOHOL WAS SOMETIMES
SMUGGLED IN ABSURD WAYS.

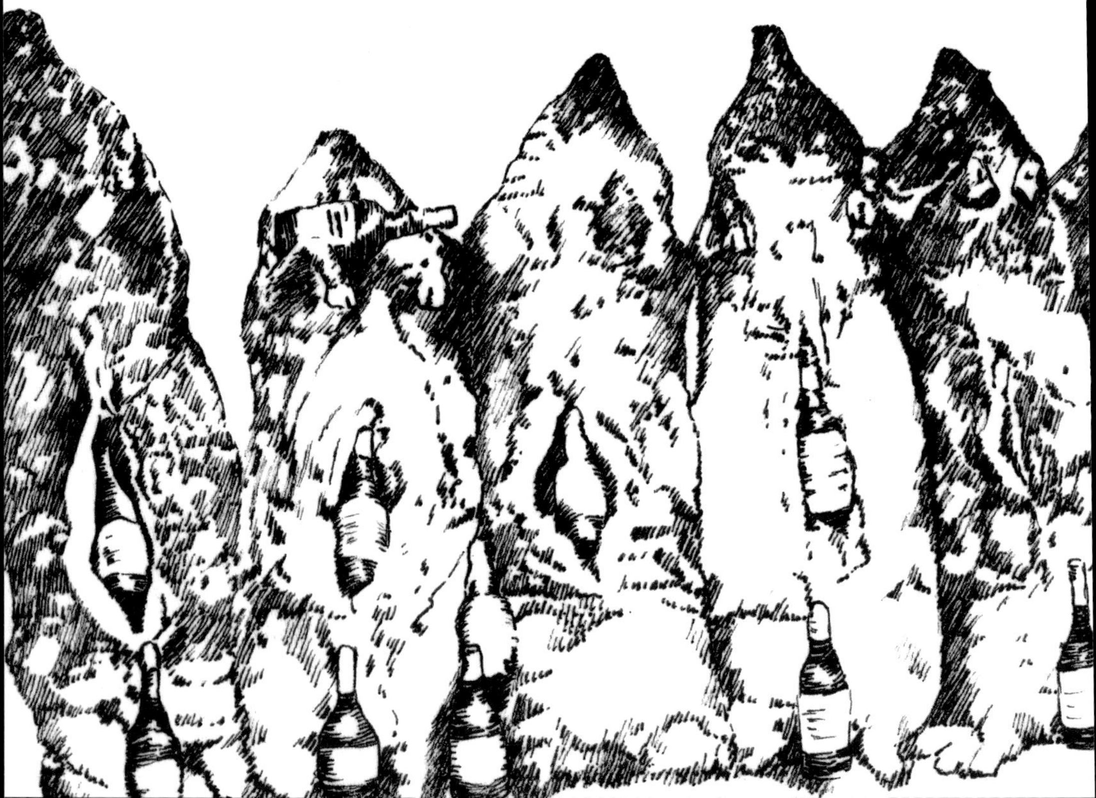

On July 16, 1916 a plebiscite to control the distribution of alcohol in the province of Alberta was successful and became law. The main pressure to create this law came from the Women's Christian Temperance Union (WCTU) and the Moral Reform League (MRL — later known as the Social Service League) in Alberta.

The WCTU was first organized in Canada in Owen Sound, Ontario in 1874. In 1905 the movement spread to the newly formed provinces of Alberta and Saskatchewan. At this time a majority of crimes were directly connected to the consumption of alcohol. Women and children were not legally protected against abusive husbands and fathers. Women did not have the right to vote or inherit property. If they escaped an abusive marriage they could be arrested and forced to return to the relationship.

The APP

WITHIN THE WCTU, activists such as Nellie McClung believed that if consumption of alcohol could be controlled, social conditions within the province would be much improved. Nellie McClung was typical of members of the wctu. The leaders of the movement were well educated and belonged to the privileged class of society. Though they did not have the vote, they exacted pressure on the powers that be in the province through their husbands and family connections.

From its inception, it was impossible to enforce Prohibition. At the time, local police forces were depleted because many men had joined the armed services to fight in World War I. Also, the territories that the force patrolled were enormous. However, having secured "their law" the wctu and mrl agitated the government for a special commission to enforce Prohibition. As a direct result of this commission, on March 1, 1917 the Alberta Provincial Police (app) was created.

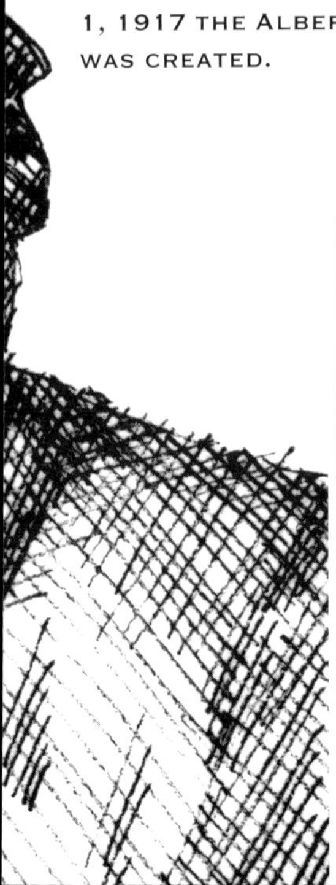

The APP — also known as "the dry squad" — was small and had limited resources. It faced the arduous task of controlling the distribution of illegal substances. This was made all the more difficult by many loopholes in the law — initially during prohibition citizens could purchase alcohol through liquor prescriptions acquired from a druggist. Bogus prescriptions abounded.

The Crowsnest Pass was the most serious trouble spot in the province — stills, speak-easies or blind pigs, as drinking establishments were sometimes called — proliferated. Concealed weapons were commonly carried and the large population of single men meant that fights often broke out at drinking establishments. Also, the majority of the population were from cultures where alcohol was integrated into daily life.

In 1921, the newly appointed attorney-general of Alberta, J.E. Brownlee, responded to increased pressure to control alcohol by enlisting fifty recruits into the APP. One of its new members was Stephen O. Lawson (right). He had emigrated from England in 1903 at the age of twenty-three. Before fighting in WWI, he had been a rancher and a member of several police forces in southern Alberta. Shortly after joining the APP in March, 1922 he was stationed at Coleman, a small town just west of Blairmore.

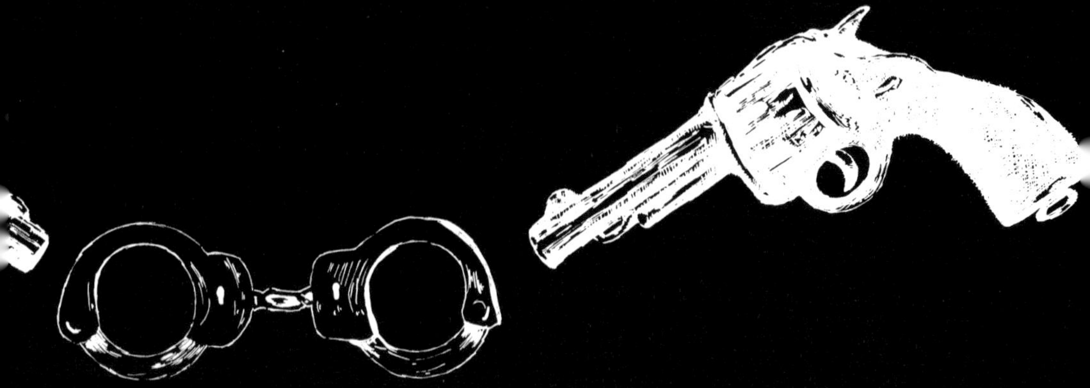

A PROVINCIAL POLICE

Many people in the province did not take the liquor laws seriously. Police officers, judges and government officials were known to routinely purchase or make illegal alcohol. Some of those in power received large payments of cash from established bootleggers and they enjoyed the growing wealth generated by the sale of alcohol.

Despite Prohibition's limitations and problems with enforcement, the Social Service League kept up a steady pressure on the government for stricter laws and higher penalties to be paid by bootleggers.

The Shooting

In the late afternoon of September 21, 1922 Emilio Picariello drives up to his hotel in Blairmore.
At the hotel he finds two APP officers, Sergeant Scott and Corporal Day. They have a search warrant. The officers have been informed that Emilio Picariello and his son Steve are returning to Blairmore with a shipment of liquor from their supplier in Fernie "Mr. Big". Acting quickly, Emilio honks the horn of his car, warning Steve that the police are there. Steve is driving the car laden with liquor.
Hearing the horn he turns the heavily loaded car around and heads back towards the BC border.
APP officers Scott and Day pursue the speeding car.
The police officers make a brief stop at a cafe on the edge of town. They telephone ahead to APP headquarters in Coleman to warn Constable Stephen Lawson that Picariello's son is heading his way with an illegal load of booze.
Constable Lawson runs into the street. He sees Steve's car approaching. He stretches out his hand for the car to stop.

Steve ignores the signal. Constable Lawson jumps out of the way as the speeding car whizzes past.
Constable Lawson aims his gun and fires. The car does not stop. However one of the bullets has hit and injures Steve in the hand.
Emilio Picariello returned home to the Alberta Hotel. At approximately 6pm, he receives a telephone call informing him that his son has been injured and is in custody at the hospital in Michel. Emilio decides to drive to Coleman to APP headquarters. He intends to discuss his son's situation with Constable Lawson.
Florence is also concerned about Steve. She asks to accompany Emilio. He asks Florence to bring along his .32 calibre handgun.
Florence retrieves the gun and they depart for Coleman.
Florence and Emilio arrive in Coleman in early evening. They slowly drive down main street towards APP headquarters.

They stop the car in front of the small house beside the Miners' Hospital. The house serves as both the police office and home to Constable Lawson and his family.
Constable Lawson is just finishing dinner. He hears Emilio call and leaves the table to go outside. He approaches the car and rests his foot on the running board while talking to Picariello.
Suddenly a struggle begins.
A series of shots are fired. Constable Lawson falls to the ground dying.

Emilio and Florence flee Coleman. They drive at top speed back towards Blairmore.

The Trial

PICARIELLO OFFERED NO RESISTANCE WHEN POLICE TOOK HIM INTO CUSTODY

First Words the Murder Suspect Asked the Officers Were Concerning His Son, Witnesses Testify.— "How's My Boy," He Inquired—No Indication Given by McKinley Cameron As to Line Defense Will Follow in Presenting Case.

The story of the search for the two accused, Emilio Picariello and Florence Lasandro, following the murder of Constable Lawson, and the arrest of Picariello on the top of the hill back of the cement plant in Blairmore, constituted the principal evidence given at the Thursday morning session of the murder trial before Mr. Justice Walsh.

A number of witnesses were examined, and it is expected the case for the prosecution will be closed by the time adjournment comes on Thursday afternoon. Sergt. Scott, of the A.P.P., one of the principal witnesses for the crown, will be called Thursday afternoon, and it is likely his examination will last for some considerable time.

As yet no indication has been given by the counsel for the defence as to what his defence will be. It is not even known how many witnesses will be called, though it is presumed the defence will not be a lengthy one.

Story of Arrest

According to the evidence of Constables E. Clarke and C. Tutin, both of the Royal Canadian Mounted Police, Picariello did not offer any resistance when, along with Constable Bradner, of the A.P.P., the accused was arrested. Both officers testified that they were sent from Lethbridge to take a part in the hunt for Picariello, [illegible] detailed to search the Italian [illegible] com-

"dead."
in Michel
Q. We
A. Con
riello if
son that
swered
then sa
give La
Picariel
me."
Q. A
A. W
woman
he had
found
Mr.
no con
arrest
A.

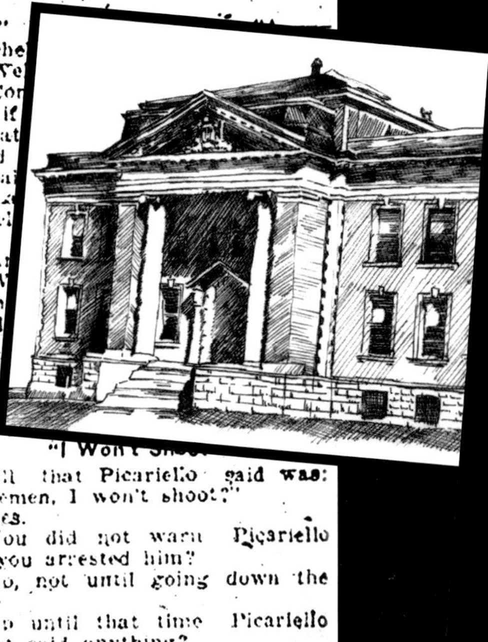

"I Won't Shoot"

Q. All that Picariello said was: "Gentlemen, I won't shoot?"
A. Yes.
Q. You did not warn Picariello when you arrested him?
A. No, not until going down the hill.
Q. Up until that time Picariello had not said anything?
A. No.
Q. Did you make any notes when Picariello made this statement?
A. No.
Q. You had your notebook?
A. Yes.

Asked After Son

[illegible] the first words Picarl-

PICARIELLO TRIAL OPENS IN CALGARY COURT ON MONDAY

Exhibits, Including Auto and Pistol Have Been Sent Here

Arrangements for the trial of Emilio Picariello and Florence Lassandro, which will open before Mr. Justice Walsh in the supreme court in Calgary next Monday morning, have been practically completed. Attorney-General J. E. Brownlee is expected back from the east either on Wednesday ... Thursday, when it is said the p... murder charge wi... A. McGillival... the case ... Sheriff ... called f... of whic... crown ... Picar...

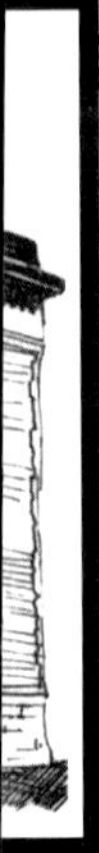

Nov. 28 1922

LITTLE DAUGHTER OF S. O. LAWSON TESTIFIES IN THE PICARIELLO MURDER TRIAL

13-Year-Old Peggy Gives Evidence Clearly, but Breaks Down and Sobs When Describing Tragic Scene—J. A. McAlpine, Who Was Picariello's Mechanic, A. Dorenzo, Who Found Deserted Car, and Others Also Among the Witnesses Tuesday Morning.

"Peggy" Lawson, the thirteen-year-old daughter of the late Constable Stephen O. Lawson, for whose murder Emilio Picariello and Florence Lasandro are facing trial in the provincial court house before Mr. Justice Walsh, was the principal witness for the prosecution on Tuesday morning. The child gave her evidence in a clear voice except when she attempted ... that she did following the hearing of the shots which had ... th to her father. At this juncture the child, after striving ... the tears, broke down and sobbed. Scores of women, ... in entering the court room, were palpably affected and ... used freely to stop the welling tears. ... however, recovered her composure and throughout her ... on, which lasted for approximately thirty minutes, she ... ements and the events of the night of the tragedy. Despite ... McKinley Cameron, K.C., subjected the child to a cross- ... or an hour, the child would not be drawn away from her ...

...Addresses Child

...ggy was allowed to be ... Justice Walsh addressed ... u know the difference be... lling the truth and a false... to which the child answered ... ffirmative. ... ou know where you go if you ... ell the truth? ... Down below. ... go to Sunday school and ... are told about God?"

... What time was this conver... sation with Picariello?

A. About 6 o'clock.

Q. Did you think his instructions had any importance to this tragedy?

A. No.

Q. You might have told the police. Being an honest boy you would have told the police?

A. Yes.

Q. You had a job with Picariello?

A. Yes.

Q. Afterwards a difference?

A. Not directly with Picariello.

Q. With his solicitors?

Q. ... not using you ...

JURY IS SECURED IN TRIAL OF PICARIELLO AND MRS. F. LASANDRO, ACCUSED OF MURDER

Counsel of Crown and Defence Put Candidates Through a Grilling Before Panel Is Completed—J. E. Bull Quizzed Respecting Christian Guardian and Excused — C. B. Adshead Is Also Excused Having Expressed Opinion Regarding Outcome.

PICARIELLO CASE ...

Following is the jury th... Picariello and Florence Lasa... Constable S. O. Lawson: ... W. H. Edge, W. L. Loc... ...ley, Leslie H. Irwin and ...

...ilio Picariello and Florence La... of murdering Constable Stephen ... mber 21 when the charge was r... riminal court, with Mr. Justice ... n Monday morning. ... The entire morning was occupied wi... and no less than forty-eight were called b...

C. H. Adshead Challenged

McKinley Cameron, K.C., senior ... nsel for the defense, after ex... ting his pre-emptory challenges, ... enged Cecil H. Adshead for ... At this juncture but two jury... had been selected and after ... g the section of the Jury Act, ... stice Walsh instructed the two ... ler judgment as to whether ... was indifferent as between ... and the accused. ... veloped that Adshead, who ... arage at Didsbury, admitted ... ad been an intimate friend ... n's and had expressed an ... friends that it was unfair ... Adshead, should be asked ... e jury. He was excused. ... es was also challenged for ... as J. E. Bull, J. W. Pen... W. Wills, and all were ...

Guardian Menti...

CHILD SAYS MRS. LASANDRO OPENED FIRE ON LAWSON AS LATTER CLASPED PICARIELLO

Murdered Constable's Nine-Year-Old Daughter Describes Shooting As She Saw It—Did Not See Picariello Shoot

Other Witnesses Testify to Hearing the Reports and Ernest Hines Swears He Saw the Prisoners Together About 7 o'Clock in the Evening Tragedy Occurred.

Positive evidence that Florence Lasandro opened fire upon her daddy

In the Supreme Court of Alberta,

Appellate Division.

The King

v.

Emilio Picarielle
and Florence Losandra

Transcript of evidence given at the trial of the charge tried at a sittings of the Supreme Court of Alberta held at Calgary, Alberta, beginning on the 27th day of November, 1922, the Honourable Mr. Justice Walsh presiding with a Jury.

VOLUME 1.

A. A. McGillivray, Esq., K. C.,
J. D. Matheson, Esq., and   appeared for the Crown.
S. J. Helman, Esq.,

[illegible] McKinely Cameron, Esq., K. C.,
[illegible] Esq., and   [illegible]ppeared for the accused.

Royal Canadian Mounted Police

"K" Division
Lethbridge.

Ref. No.

East Kootenay Sub-District
Michel Detachment.
Sept. 23rd. 1922.

File
/4944

Report.

Re. Emil Picareille. Alleged Murderer.

On the 21st instant, about 9.15 P.M. I received a telephone message from Inspt. Bruce at. Fernie, B.C. to the affect, that Const Lawson of the Alberta Provincial Police at Coleman, Alta had been shot and killed by one Emil Picareillo "Italian" and that a woman one Mrs. Lasandra was supposed to be with him at the time of the shooting.

My instructions were, to be on the look-out for both parties, and prevent their escape through Michel.

Immediatly after receiveing these instructions, Regt. No. 7763 Const Schlesinger T. and myself covered both the main trails and C.P.R. tracks consistently until the news of Picareillo's and the woman's arrest at Blairmore, Alta. at 7.20 P.M. of the 22nd. inst.

During the afternoon of the 22nd. instant Regt. No. 5725 Corpl. Smith A.E., arrived from Blairmore and assisted until the news of the arrest. Cpl. Smith left on the 23rd inst. on train for Fernie.

S.H. Moseley
(S.H. Moseley) Const.
Regt. No. 6093
In charge of Michel Detachment.

The Officer Commanding,
Lethbridge, Alta.

Forwarded.

W.V. Bruce
Insp.
W. V. Bruce
27-9-22. Commander East Kootenay Sub Dist

Picariel
Sente
On

ity of Murder," Is
Charged with Slayin
Coleman

MR. JUSTICE
IN DEC

Prisoners Hear Sentenc
And Are Entrained
Evening—Ju

Attorney-General's Charge

Hon. J. E. Brownlee, attorney-general, addressed the court to the effect that he was appearing personally in order to prefer the charge of murder against the two accused. He also submitted authority for the appointment of A. A. McGillivray, K.C., as senior counsel for the prosecution.

Prisoners in Dock

Picariello and the Lasandro woman as they sat side by side in the prisoners' dock, presented a striking contrast. Picariello, dressed in a navy blue suit, with tie to match, clean-shaven and with moustache neatly trimmed, talked freely with his coun-

... and smiled several times during ... proceedings. He showed signs of ...vousness on a few occasions and with his handkerchief would wipe his forehead. Florence Lasandro, on the other hand, seemed pale and worn and did not speak during the session except to answer "Not guilty" when the charge was read.

Mistake at Prel

Witness at this poi... he made a mistake in g... at the preliminary hea... said one of the guns wa... revolver. It should ha... calibre, but he had be... its size.

Mr. Cameron: I thi... another mistake. Did ... you did not look for th... at the preliminary?

A. I don't think I di... looked for it.

Mr. Cameron read ... dence given at that t... that the witness had m... statement.

Q. Did you take any ... search?

A. None.

and Lasandro
ed to Be Hanged
bruary Twenty-first

t Returned Against Couple
nstable S. O. Lawson at
a, September 21

SH CONCURS
N OF TRIAL JURY

unced at 8:08 p.m. Saturday
e of Execution the Same
About Four Hours

"PIC" TRIAL COST ALBERTA JUST $15,000

The cost to the province of Alberta of the Picariello trial, from the time of the murder of Constable Lawson until conviction of his slayers, was $15,000, according to information furnished The Herald by crown authorities. This includes cost of investigation, remuneration to witnesses for loss of time, counsel's fees, traveling expenses and other costs incidental to the conduct of the case, but does not include salaries of police officers, of whom there were a host employed in the case, or salaries of other officials.

that
ence
he
libre
.38
by

nade
that
tion

inly

evi-
wing
uch

your

Despite the close cross-examination to which Mr. Cameron subjected Joseph Plante, witness maintained the shooting came from the inside of the car. Witness had declared that the flashes came from the "off" side of the car, and Mr. Cameron endeavored to find out just what the witness meant by "off."

"He got over into British C
about 5 o'clock on the afternoo
21st. According to evidence
some people regarding the sho
Coleman that afternoon, Piccar
'If he shot my boy I'll kill hir
night, by God,' and kissed h
Another version of it was that
'I'll shoot every G— d— polic
the Pass,' and then drew his
kissed it. Between 5 and 6 o'
Blairmore, George Allen met hir
street and Piccarillo said, 'I h
have shot my boy. I don't l
shooting business, and if they

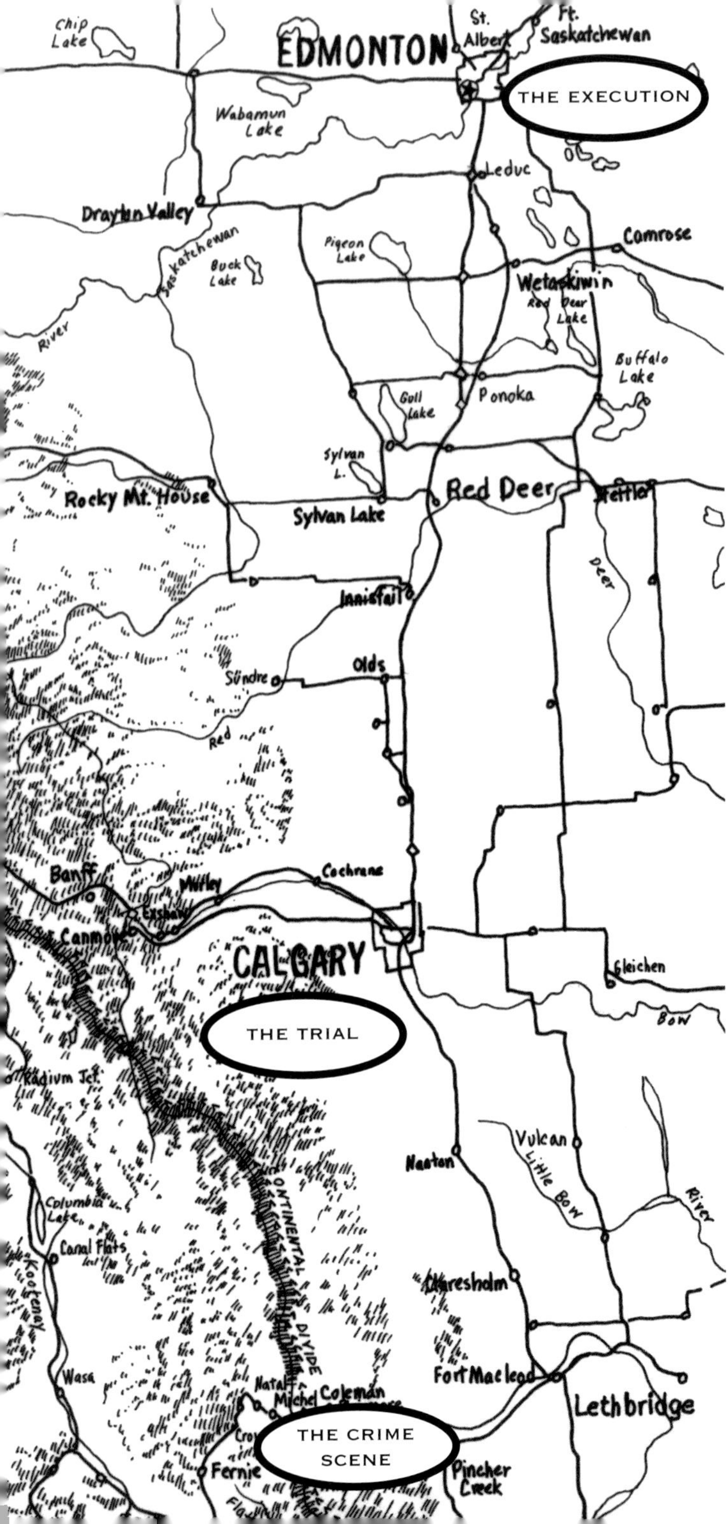

Chip Lake
EDMONTON
St. Albert
Ft. Saskatchewan
THE EXECUTION
Wabamun Lake
Leduc
Drayton Valley
Saskatchewan
Buck Lake
Pigeon Lake
Camrose
Wetaskiwin
Red Deer Lake
River
Buffalo Lake
Gull Lake
Ponoka
Sylvan L.
Rocky Mt. House
Red Deer
Sylvan Lake
Deer
Innisfail
Olds
Sundre
Red
Banff
Cochrane
Exshaw
Canmore
CALGARY
Gleichen
Bow
THE TRIAL
Radium Jct.
Vulcan
Little Bow
River
Nanton
Columbia Lake
Canal Flats
CONTINENTAL DIVIDE
Kootenay
Claresholm
Wasa
Natal
Michel
Coleman
Fort Macleod
Lethbridge
THE CRIME SCENE
Fernie
Pincher Creek

PROVINCIAL GAOL, LETHBRIDGE, ALTA.

When corresponding with prisoners you must write in English, your letters will be opened and examined by the Warden. You write as often as you wish. Prisoners may write once a month. Wednesday is visiting day between 1 and 3 p.m. [redacted] Tobacco and Chewing Gum are prohibited. [redacted] visitors received on Sundays or Public Holidays.

Please mail this letter

To [write plainly] Mrs Picariello
Blairmore
Alta

Address your answer

To [prisoner's name]

Box 848
Lethbridge,
Alberta.

Oct 29th

Dear Wife and Family
I just write this flew line to let you know if our boy Steve do not get any beter I want you to get him to Coleman Hospital he will be take care there and du at once if is necessary I do not want to get our local Dr. I don't like him he is a forny
Dear Wife write soon and how the other kids and Angiolina, I recived e letter our boy Carmine wrote soon Charl Comes back let me know. Mr. Gillis come up Sarderday and everthin goin good. give my best regarde to our frinds also Filumena, give my best love and kisses to our Children
Your loving Husband
and Father
E Picariello

Florence's Appeal

Mrs. Lasandro Declares "Pic" Was Actual Slayer

Special Dispatch to The Herald)

FERNIE, B. C., May 1. — Mrs. Vincenzo Constanza, of this city, returned a few days ago from Fort Saskatchewan, where she visited her daughter, Florence Lasandro, who, with Picariello, is under sentence to die on the scaffold at that place on May 2, for the murder of S. O. Lawson, at Coleman, last September.

Mrs. Constanza states her daughter has now made a sworn confession of her part of the crime. The statement of the Lasandro woman as related by the mother is startling in different respects. It introduces another woman as an eye witness to the tragedy, whose name is alleged to be Mrs. Joseph Filfile. This woman insofar as the proceedings heretofore are concerned has never been mentioned.

Guided By Husband

Florence Lasandro's story, according to her mother, is that she has maintained absolute silence until now upon advice, being particularly so guided by the influence of her husband, James Lasandro, who resides at Blairmore, and who is in the employ of Picariello and has been for some time.

In Shadow of Gallows

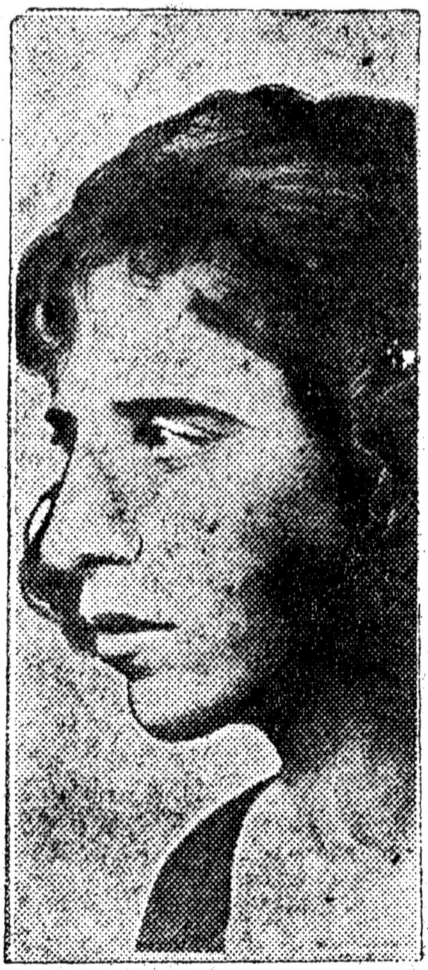

Mrs. Florence Lassandra, who awaits death on the gallows with Emile Piccarillo on Wednesday, for the killing of a policeman. Final efforts are now being made to have her sentence commuted to life imprisonment. See also Page 7.

A Canadian Press despatch at 2 p.m. states that the appeal of the Canadian Prisoners' Welfare Association on behalf of the woman has been received by the Prime Minister. It will be placed before the Privy Council.

CAPITAL CASE.

23118

Year 1922

Department of the Secretary of State

CANADA.

…e of Trial Judge The Honourable Mr. Justice Walsh,
…ess Calgary, Alta.
…of Report December 4th, 1922
…f Receipt December 9th, 1922

SUBJECT:

…n Capital Case of (EMELIO PICARIELLO (FLORENCE LASSANDRO

…d for Execution: 21st day of February, 1923.

Ottawa, December 11th, 1922

…d to the Honourable the Minister of Justice for his …n.

BY COMMAND,

UNDER-SECRETARY OF STATE.

FORM T. D. 65

CANADIAN PACIFIC RAILWAY COMPANY'S TELEGRAPH

PRESS DESPATCH

1.MO. Y. 118 4 NL. NIGHT LETTER---2EX. 3AM APRIL29TH-

COUNT PNS AND DASHES.

EDMONTON ALTA APL 28 29 1923

MINISTER OF JUSTICE,

OTTAWA, ONT.

FOLLOWING VOLUNTARY STATEMENT MADE IN WRITING AND SIGNED BY FLORENCE LOSANDRO IN THE PRESENCE OF HER SPIRITUAL ADVISOR AND PROVINCIAL GOVERNMENT OFFICIALS CALLED AT HER REQUEST TODAY, SATURDAY THE TWENTY - EIGHTH, IS HEREBY TRANSMITTED TO YOU AT HER REQUEST;

QUOTE; MR PICARIELLO WENT TO FERNIE ON THE DAY OF SHOOTING WITH HIS WIFE, SON AND ANOTHER GIRL, FOR LIQUOR AS HE TOLD ME STOP HE CAME HOME ABOUT 4,30 I HEARD HIM SAY THE POLICEMAN ARE AFTER ME. STOP. HE CALLED HIS SON OUT AND SAID WHEN YOU HEAR ME WHISTLE YOU BEAT IT BACK TO BC WITH THE LOAD. STOP. I KNEW THAT THE BOY HAD GONE. STOP ABOUT 6 PM I HEARD THAT THE BOY HAD BEEN SHOT GOING THROUGH COLEMAN STOP. ABOUT TWENTY TO SEVEN THE BOY CALLED UP THROUGH THE PHONE FROM MICHEL. I ANSWERED THE PHONE. STOP. HE ASKED FOR HIS FATHER WHO CAME TO THE PHONE AND TALKED TO THE BOY. STOP. I HEARD HIM SAY CAN YOU DRIVE BACK. STOP. I DONT KNOW WHAT THE ANSWER WAS BUT HEARD MR PICARIELLO SAY HE WOULD DRIVE UP TO BRING HIM BACK. STOP. HE WENT OUT, GOT IN THE CAR AND I WENT

FORM T. D. 65

CANADIAN PACIFIC RAILWAY COMPANY'S TELEGRAPH

1 . MO. Y.---

PRESS DESPATCH

2ND SHEET--HON MIN OF JUSTICE, FROM EDMONTON ALTA APRIL 28TH.

WITH HIM AT HIS REQUEST IN ORDER THAT I MIGHT BRING THE BOY'S (STEVE) CAR BACK. STOP HE TOLD ME TO GET A GUN. I WENT TO MY HUSBAND'S TRUNK AND GOT THE GUN AND SOME BULLETS. STOP. WE WENT TO COLEMAN. WE DID NOT TALK ON THE WAY STOP. WHEN THERE WE STOPPED AT A HOTEL AND HE HAD A CONVERSATION WITH A MAN, WHO TOLD HIM HIS BOY WAS SHOT BUT THAT HE DID NOT THINK HE

WAS BADLY HURT. STOP. HE DROVE TO CORNER OF MAIN STREET AND TURNED BACK TOWARD LAWSON'S PLACE STOP. HE STOPPED CAR IN FRONT OF HOUSE, DOOR OF WHICH WAS OPEN. STOP. I SAW A MAN INSIDE. PICARIELLO CALLED TO HIM AND HE CAME OUT AND SAID YES SIR. STOP. PICARIELLO SAID DO YOU KNOW THAT YOU HAVE SHOT MY BOY HE ANSWERED "OH DO I" MR PICARIELLO PUT ONE ARM ON BACK OF SEAT AND THE OTHER ON STEERING WHEEL AND LAWSON LEANED FORWARD ON DOOR OF CAR. STOP THEY TALKED BUT NOT IN AN EXCITED WAY. I WAS NOT PAYING MUCH ATTENTION AND ALL AT ONCE I HEARD TWO SHOTS. STOP. I TURNED AROUND AND AS I DID.

FORM T. D. 65

CANADIAN PACIFIC RAILWAY COMPANY'S TELEGRAPH

PRESS DESPATCH

1. MO Y.----

HON MIN JUSTICE, FROM EDMONTON, APRIL28TH.

THIRD SHEET- --

SO I SAW A FLASH GO OVER MY LEGS AND SAW LAWSON ON TOP OF PICARIELLO WITH HIS ARM AROUND HIS NECK AND STRUGGLING FOR A GUN. DONT KNOW IN WHOSE HAND GUN WAS. STOP. I SCREAMED GOT ON MY KNEES, GOT HOLD OF SOME ONES HANDS, - I DONT KNOW WHOSE, STOP. THE GUN WENT OFF AGAIN. STOP. AFTER THAT I SAW TWO FLASHES IN THE ALLAY AND NEXT THING I SAW WAS LAWSON LYING ON HIS BACK IN THE ALLEY STOP. THE GUN THEY WERE STRUGGLING FOR WAS NOT THE ONE I BROUGHT BUT ONE THAT I SUPPOSED BELONGED TO PICARIELLO. I DONT KNOW WHAT BECOME OF THAT STOP. I WENT BACK TO BLAIRMORE IN THE CAR I WENT TO A LITTLE SHACK THERE AND STAYED THERE WITH PICARIELLO THE GREATER PART OF THE NIGHT STOP. WE DISCUSSED THE MATTER TOGETHER AND I ASK HIM HOW IT HAPPENED . HE SAID I DONT KNOW STOP. I ASKED HIM IF IT COULD HAVE HAPPENED WHEN I STRUCK HIS HAND UP. HE SAID IT MIGHT HAVE FOR ME TO TAKE THE BLAME AS WOMEN DONT HANG IN CANADA THAT WHEN HE WOULD GET OUT HE WOULD SPEND THE LAST CENT HE

FORM T

CANADIAN PACIFIC RAILWAY COMPANY'S TELEGRAPH

1. MO Y.--

PRESS DESPATCH

FOURTH SHEET----- HON MIN JUSTICE, FROM EDMONTON APL28TH

HAD TO GET ME OUT STOP. I NEVER TOUCHED THE GUN IN THE CAR STOP JUST ASTER WE LEFT LAWSON PICARIELLO SAID OH MY GOD WHAT DID I DO. STOP. AFTER WE GOT OUT OF THE CAR AT BLAIRMORE HE GAVE ME THE GUN FOR MY OWN PROTECTION. STOP. ON OUR WAY BACK FROM COLEMAN, PICARIELLO APPEARED TO BE DAZED AND I HAD TO HELP HOM WITH THE STEERING WHEEL HE SEEMED HELPLESS. STOP. HE ASKED ME TO LOAD THE GUN FOR HIM BUT I SAID I DONT KNOW HOW. HE THEN LOADED IT WHILE I HELD THE STEERING WHEEL. STOP. I WENT OUT WITH PICARIELLO AND THE SON FOR PROTECTION IN ORDER THAT I MIGHT SAY IT WAS MY BOOZE AND I WOULD TAKE THE BLAME. STOP. HE SAID THEY WOULD NOT FIRE ON A CAR WITH A WOMAN IN IT. STOP. MY HUSBAND WAS WORKING FOR PICARIELLO AND WE ALL LIVED TOGETHER AS ONE FAMILY HE TREATED ME AS A DAUGHTER. STOP. I SAW PICARIELLO ARRESTED WHEN I WAS IN A HOUSE OF HIS KRMM FRIEND NEARBY STOP. I SAID TO THE WOMAN IN THE HOUSE, I MIGHT AS WELL GIVE MYSELF UP. SHE SAID YES, AND WE AGREED.

?

FORM T. D. 65

CANADIAN PACIFIC RAILWAY COMPANY'S TELEGRAPH

1. MO Y.

PRESS DESPATCH

SHEET FIVE----- HON MIN MM JUSTICE, FROM EDMONTON APL28TH.

THAT IT WOULD BE BEST FOR ME TO TAKE THE RESPONSIBILITY AND SAY THAT I DID IT AS WOMEN DONT HANG IN CANADA AND HE WOULD GET OFF. STOP. I NEVER HEARD OF LAWSON BEFORE THE SHOOTING-DAD NOT KNOW WHERE HE LIVED AND ON THE WAY TO COLEMAN WE NEVER DISCUSSED HIM STOP. I DID NOT KNOW UNTIL AFTERWARD THAT HE HAD SHOT STEVE I ONLY CARED FOR STEVE AS A BROTHER AND HAD NO REASON FOR REVENGE STOP. LAWSON WAS SHOT BY A THIRTY EIGHT REVOLVER BUT

I DONT KNOW HOW IT HAPPENED. I AM POSITIVE THAT
I NEVER HAD A GUN IN MY HANDS. STOP. HE
ALSO TOLD ME TO SAY IN CASE HIS FINGER PRINTS
WERE SHOWN ON THE THRRTY - EIGHT THAT I SHOULD SAY
THAT I GAVE IT TO HIM TO LOAD AND THAT
HE LOADED IT FOR ME. I DID NOT KNOW HOW
TO SHOOT A GUN AND WHEN HE HANDED ME THE
THIRTY - EIGHT AFTER LEAVING COLEMAN I TOLD HIM I
DID NOT KNOW HOW TO SHOOT A GUN. HE SAID
JUST PULL THE TRIGGER STOP. I NEVER SHOT A GUN
IN MY LIFE. - WAS ALWAYS AFRAID OF THEM STOP
ON THE

FORM T. D. 65

CANADIAN PACIFIC RAILWAY COMPANY'S TELEGRAPH

PRESS DESPATCH

1.MO .Y.
SHEET SIX----- HON MIN JUSTICE, FROM EDMONTON APRIL 28TH.

WAY TO COLEMAN HE WAS TALKING TO
HIMSELF AND I HEARD HIM SAY I'LL SHOOT THE SON
OF A BITCH I TOLD FATHER FIDELIS SOME TWO MONTHS
AGO THAT I WAS INNOCENT. STOP. I TOLD HARRIS, MY
FIRST SOLICITOR, THAT I HAD AGREED TO TAKE ALL BLAME
BUT I NEVER MENTIONED THIS TO CAMERON. PICARIELLO TOLD ME
TO SAY AS LITTLE AS POSSIBLE AND HE WOULD DO
THE TALKING. STOP. WHILE WE WERE NEARING LAWSON'S HOUSE, I
NOTICED THAT MAN IN HOUSE WAS A POLICEMAN - COULD TELL
THAT BY HIS BREECHES. I SAID TO PICARIELLO WHATEVER YOU
DO DO NOT SHOOT. HE MADE NO REPLY. AFTERWARD HE
SAYS YOU TELL ANYONE WHO ASKS YOU THAT YOU DID
IT AND IF ANYONE TELLS YOU THAT I HAVE CONFESSED
TELL THEM THAT THEY ARE DAMN LIARS. HE WAS TO
TELL THE SAME STORY. STOP. FOREGOING STATEMENT IS MADE BY
ME VOLUNTARILY, TAKEN DOWN AT MY REQUEST TO BE USED
FOR TRANSMISSION TO MINISTER OF JUSTICE OTTAWA OR OTHERWISE AS MY
SPIRITUAL ADVISOR MAY SEE FIT(SIGNED) FLORENCE LOSANDRO. QUOTATIONS
STOP.

J.E.BROWNLEE, ATTORNEY GENERAL. 320AM.

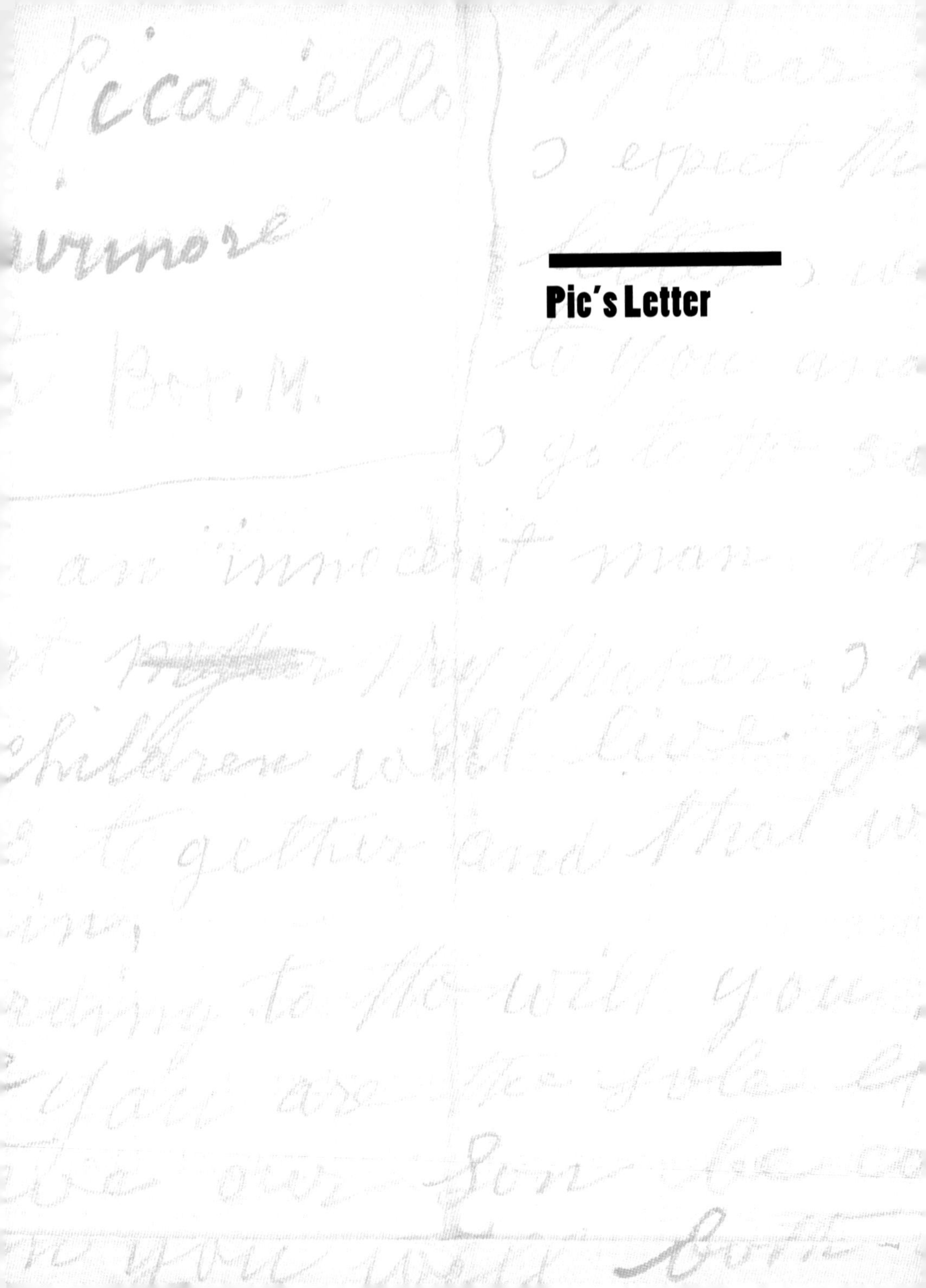

Piccariello

urmore

Box M.

My Dear

I expect the

to you and

I go to the

am innocent man

children will live

together and that

to the will you

our Son

Pic's Letter

[May 11, 1923]

to Mrs. Piccariello
Blairmore
alta Box. M.

My dear wife and children
I expect this will be the last letter I will be abel to write to you and the children
I go to the scaffold to morrow morning as an innocent man. and I am prepared to meet ~~my~~ my Maker. I hope that you and the children will live good and happy lives to gether and that we will all meet again,
according to the will you have already from me you are the sole excicutrix until Steve our son be comes of age and then you will both be come the trustees ~~with you~~. and I wish that they all get an equal share
I want you to know that I do not owe any body, [redacted] I want you to know that Mr. E. Gillis as already had $4500.00 from me and I consider I have over paid him for work that he had never done, all others lawyers are paid in full

May 11th. 1923

over

(2) I want you to know that I did not authorize dor. Oliver to attend any body professionally out side of our own family. I want you to remember all the people I have helped at different times they have forgotten me now. and dont come to help or cheer me

I will say good bye with love to you all children til we all meet again and may God Bless and keep you all safe kis all the children for me

Your loving Husband

And Father

Emilio Piariello

P.S.

My Brother and my mother. new adress

viale Platani

propietà margherito

Avellino

Italy

The Execution

Picariello and Lasa
Die on Gallows;
Their Innocen

"You Are Hanging an Innocent Man—God Help Me," and Picariello Waves Black Cap Aside — "Why Do You Hang Me When I Didn't Do Anything?" —Lasandro

CONDEMNED PAIR MEET DEATH JUST AFTER SUNRISE TODAY

Both Prisoners Mount Gallows in Good Mental and Physical Condition After Good Night and Normal Breakfast Woman Displays Greatest Fortitude Throughout

(By Canadian Press)

FORT SASKATCHEWAN, May 2.—The double hanging of Emilio Picariello and Mrs. Florence Lasandro, convicted murderers of Provincial Constable S. O. Lawson, at Coleman, Alta., last September, was carried out in Fort Saskatchewan penitentiary at daylight this morning. Picariello paid the penalty at 5.10 and Mrs. Lasandro at 5.51.

Both protested their innocence to the last.

Mrs. Lasandro is the first woman to be hanged in Canada for 24 years and the fifth since Confederation.

Emilio Picariello and his accomplice, Mrs. Florence Lasandro, spent the last night of their lives in a resigned condition at the provincial jail at Fort Saskatchewan, before going to the gallows this morning.

Just before dying, Picariello said: "You are hanging an innocent man—God help me." His request to the priest was that the black cap not be put over his eyes but, of course, this was not permitted as the prison authorities had no authority for such action.

Mrs. Lasandro's statement on the scaffold was: "Why do you hang me when I didn't do anything? Is there anyone here who has any pity?" Just before the trap was sprung she forgave everybody.

No disposition has been made of the bodies as yet.

ro
otest
to Last

Some Petitions Asked That Law Take Its Course

(By Canadian Press)

OTTAWA, May 2. — Petitions to the government in the Picariello-Lasandro double hanging case were marked by unusual circumstances. While on the one hand, there were the customary pleas for clemency, especially in the case of the woman, petitions were also received, it is stated, urging that the law should be permitted to take its full course. Representations against clemency are very unusual, especially in the case of a condemned woman, and the signatories in some cases were women.

Both cases had long consideration before the cabinet and it was not till last night that Sir Lomer Gouin, minister of justice, announced final decision.

La Tribun

ANNO XIII PREZZO 2 soldi Toronto Ont. S

La Doppia Inpiccagione In Alberta, e la Proibizione

In altra parte del giornale abbiamo dato il resoconto della doppia inpiccagione avvenuta nell'Alberta di due italiani, uno dei quali una donna.
La cosa non sarebbe stata tanto nota, giacchè non è la prima volta che le impiccagioni succedono anche triplici, non di italiani, fortunatamente, se non per il fatto che una donna vi era compresa. La stampa inglese nel dare il resoconto del fatto, era tutta premurosa a far notare come fossero ben 24 anni dacchè l'ultima donna aveva salito il patibolo in Canada, e come quantunque parecchie donne siano state ni questi 24 anni condannate a morte, pure in ogni occasione grazia della vita venne sempre fatta.

Ottimamente, colleghi della stampa dicela, grazia della vita fu sempre fatta fin ora, forse perchè le condannate erano inglesi. Oggi che invece era una italiana, la grazia, che prima stata sempre fatta, viene negata, e la legge ha dobuto avere il suo corso.

Premesso, che per principio, noi siamo avversi alla pena di morteo che chiamata col nome di assassinio legale; ci domandiamo: come mai il Governo di Ottawa che ha in tante altre occasioni ritrovato i motivi per poter raccomandare al Governatore Ge[illegible] la clemenza, come mai il Dipar[illegible]ento dell'Attorney General che ha l'incarico di preparare le pratiche per la considerazione del Gabinetto, non abbino ritrovato in questa occasione una parola di raccomandazione, un semplice dubbio che giustificasse l'usanza della commutazione della pena di morte? Forse, ripetiamo perchè era italiana!

Stando a quello che i giornali hanno detto, la Lassandra non fu mai chiamata a deporre a sua difesa, e neppure il Piccarello. Entrambi avrebbero mantenuto un mutismo certo difficile a spiegarsi per persone che si dicono innocenti, e si sarebbero accontentati di quanto l'accusa provò, cioè essere stata la Lassandra a sparare i colpi fatali. Chi tace, acconsente, si suol dire e così l'avranno intesa giudici e giurati, che li condannarono entrambi.

Però giunta alle ultime 24 ore di vita, la Lassandro consia che ormai l'influenza del Piccarello non poteva salvarla, a mezzo del prete confess e annunzia ciò che dice essere la verità, e racconta come fosse stato il Piccarello, il quale sarebbe stato armato di due revolver, a sparare i colpi fatali;

Cla

Canadiana

Maggio 1923

Ufficio: 337 SHAW ST. (Rear)
Telefono College 2636

The Double Hanging in Alberta and Prohibition.

In other parts of the paper we gave an account of the double hanging of the two Italians in Alberta, one of which being a woman.

The incident would not have been so noticeable as it is not the first time that hanging was also done in triple; fortunately, not Italians, if it were not for the fact that a woman figured in the execution.

The English newspapers in giving the details of the event were eager in pointing out that it was twenty-four years since the last woman was put to the gallows in Canada, and although a number of women have been since sentenced to death, yet in each case, a pardon was granted.

In a decent way, our press colleagues say that pardon was always granted to a woman, probably because they were English, but today, because it happened to be an Italian the pardon, which before had always been granted, was denied and the law had to take its course.

We firstly state that we are adversed to capital punishment. In every civilized country is called legal murder, and we ask how is it, that the Ottawa Government, who in other occasions, found motives to warrant a plea of clemency to the Governor General. How is it, that the Attorney General Department whose duty is to prepare a reprieve for the consideration of the Cabinet has not found in this occasion a word of recommendation, or a simple doubt to commute the penalty of death? We repeat, perhaps is because she was Italian.

Other news papers have said that Lassandra was not called to testify in her own behalf, nor was Piccarello. Both, no doubt, would have maintained silence, and it would have been very difficult to ascertain who was the innocent one, but they would have been contented of the result of their trial, viz, that Lassandra fired the fatal shots.

Who maintains silence, naturally approves, and the Judge and Jury both responsible for their fate, would have at least heard if they had anything to say.

Upon reaching the last twenty-four hours of life, Lassandra, aware of the fact that Piccarello's influence could not have saved her, through the medium of a Priest confessed and declared, what is supposed to be the truth, that it was Piccarello, who, armed with two revolvers, fired the fatal shots, passing on to her, one of the revolvers to conceal and to bind her to silence.

This confession was sent to Ottawa. The Cabinet discussed it, and when this was done, the Attorney General had no other reply to give than: "We had to accomplish a painful duty. Lassandra must pay with her life for the crime she has committed. There is no evidence she can attribute to her innocence, other than she firmly states that she has not committed the crime and accuses her companion".

La Tribun

ANNO XIII PREZZO 2 soldi Toronto Ont. S

We do not intend to make any insinuations, but we simply say that we can bet 99% that if she were English, the whole matter would have taken a different aspect; a reprieve would have been granted and at the end a pardon would have been attained, but she was an Italian and more over engaged in bootlegging.

The sacred Churches and Protestant organizations, influentially in similar cases did not interceed. To be contaminated with bootlegging, there might be, perhaps, for some people, no major crime. Hence, no pity was to be shown. An example was necessary, so the lawhad to take its course.

The liberal Press and others, sent broadcast the news that the Alberta tragedy was due to the Federal law, for permitting the exportation of liquor, a trade that promotes contraband, and of which trade, it had been said, that Piccarello was attached.

We believe that our press colleagues are mistaken in so judging, and it is the idea of other people, and our firm opinion, that the fault, not only of this act, but of the flourishment of contraband, is due to the prohibition law itself; a law that the majority of the people have not approved will never approve and will not assort.

In reality, if the mass of the people wants and agrees to accept prohibition, bootleggers would go out of existence.

There cannot be vendors where there are no purchasers.

The same as all other laws wanted and imposed by the minority, prohibition will not be observed, it will be continually violated; will daily create hypocrites, perjurous; will corrupt the authority and give occasion the same as in the Picarello case, a crime which would have not happened if it were not for prohibition.

Canadiana

Maggio 1923

Ufficio: 337 SHAW ST. (Rear)
Telefono College 2636

passando quindi ad essa la rivoltella coll'ingiunzione di tacere. Questa dichiarazione viene mandata ad Ottowa, il Gabinetto la discute, ed a discussione finita, l'Attorney General non ha altra risposta da dare che: Abbiamo dovuto compiere un penoso dovere. La Lassandro deve pagare colla vita il delitto che nessuna evidenza di fatto puo ad essa attribuire, che essa dice di non aver commesso, e del quale essa fermamente accusa ora il suo compagno.

Non intendiamo fare insinuazioni, ma semplicemente diciamo, come vi sia da scomettere il 99 su cento, chè se si fosse trattata di un inglese, la cosa sarebbe stata trattata diversamente, una nuova dilazione sarebbe stata concessa, ed in fine la grazia sarebbe giunta. Ma trattavasi di una italiana, e per soppragiunta italiana mischiata ai bootlegger. Le santissime chiese ed organizzazioni protestanti, influentissime in simili casi, se ne stettero inoperose. Puzzare di bootlegg..., vi puo essere forse per tal gente, delitto maggiore? Quindi nessuna pietà doveva esse[illegible]. Un esempio era necessario, e [illegible] so.

La stampa liberale ed acquaiuola, urla ai quattro venti, come la causa principale della tragedia dell'Alberta, sia dovuta alla Legge Federale che permette il commercio di esportazione del liquore commercio che fa fiorire e sostiene il contrabbando al quale dicesi il Pirlarello era addetto.

Noi crediamo che in questo loro giudizio, i colleghi della stampa sbagliano giacchè e idea di molti, e da noi condivisa, che la sola causa di questo dramma, non solo, ma del fiorire del contrabbando del liquore, sia invece la legge di proibizione stessa; legge che il popolo nella sua maggioranza non ha approvata, non approva, e non vuole subire. Infatti se la popolazione in massa volesse la proibizione e l'accettasse, i bootlegger non esisterebbero. Non vi possono essere venditori senza compratori.

Come tutte le altre leggi volute ed imposte da una minoranza, quella della proibizione non potrà mai essere fatta osservare, essa sarà sempre continuamente violata, creando giornalmente degli ipvocriti, spergiuri; corrompendo le autorità, e dando occasione come nel caso Piccarello, ai delitti che forse non avverrebbero se non esistesse la legge di proibizione.

Sources

Sources for images are indicated within chapters by double-page spreads. GMA = Glenbow Museum Archives; LAC = Library and Archives Canada.

Front Cover

Ossessione, 1943 (dir. Luchino Visconti).

Front End Paper

GMA.

Title Page

Ossessione.

Fernie ca. 1908

GMA (*Fernie ca. 1908*). Fernie and District Historical Society. *Steerage*, 1907 (photograph by Alfred Stieglitz); *The Godfather Part II*, 1974 (dir. Francis Ford Coppola) (3). Ellis Island Foundation. Amantea family photo album; original drawing. Wayne Norton and Naomi Miller, eds., *The Forgotten Side of the Border: British Columbia's Elk Valley and Crowsnest Pass*, Kamloops: Plateau Press, 1998. GMA (2).

The Mines

GMA (*The Mines*). GMA (2) (photograph of coal face by Thomas Gushul). GMA (6); Amantea family photo album (image with handwriting).

Filumena

Amantea family photo album (*Filumena*). GMA (2); found map. *Ossessione* (2). Original drawing; Santopinto family photo album (2). Amantea family photo album; GMA; *Household Saints*, 1993 (Dir. Nancy Savoca). *Household Saints* (4). GMA. *Household Saints* (2); *Ossessione.*

Emperor Pic

GMA (*Emperor Pic*). GMA. Original drawing; GMA. *Borsalino*, 1970 (dir. Jacques Deray); GMA (5); found photograph of Al Capone; *Once Upon a Time in America*, 1984 (dir. Sergio Leone); *Racket Busters*, 1938 (dir. Lloyd Bacon); *The Godfather Part II*, 1974; *Bonnie and Clyde*, 1967 (dir. Arthur Penn); *The Roaring Twenties*, 1939 (dir. Raoul Walsh); *The Asphalt Jungle*, 1950 (dir. John Huston).

Labour and Racism

Faith Moosang, *C.D. Hoy*, Vancouver: Presentation House Gallery/Arsenal Pulp Press, 1999 (*Labour and Racism*). British Columbia Archives; *C.D. Hoy* (4). GMA (2). *C.D. Hoy* (3); GMA.

Florence and Charles

The Public Enemy, 1931 (dir. William Wellman) (*Florence and Charles*). *The Lady From Shanghai*, 1947 (dir. Orson Welles); *Al Capone*, 1959 (dir. Richard Wilson); Mark Kingwell, *Canada Our Century: 500 Visions, 100 Voices*, Toronto: Doubleday Canada, 1999; *Bonnie and Clyde* (2); *Public Enemy; Scarface*, 1932 (dir. Howard Hawks).

Prohibition

GMA (*Prohibition*). Found postcard (*A Happy New Year*); GMA (8). *The Forgotten Side*; GMA (2). GMA (2); *L'Eternel Retour*, 1943 (dir. Jean Delannoy).

The APP

GMA (*The APP*). GMA; Found postcard (Suffragette poster). GMA (2). Provincial Archives of Alberta.

The Shooting

Photograph by Lewis Hine (*The Shooting*). Photograph by Lewis Hine; *Bonnie and Clyde*; Provincial Archives of Alberta; *Canada Our Century*; GMA (2); *Heat*, 1995 (dir. Michael Mann); *Force of Evil*, 1948 (dir. Abraham Polonsky); *Bonnie and Clyde*; *High Sierra*, 1941 (dir. Raoul Walsh). GMA (4); *The Lavender Hill Mob*, 1951 (dir. Charles Crichton) (2). *Ossessione*; *Crime of Passion*, 1957 (dir. Gerd Oswald); GMA; *Night and the City*, 1950 (dir. Jules Dassin).

The Trial

Galt Museum and Archives, Lethbridge (*The Trial*). Calgary Herald Archives; Galt Museum and Archives. Photograph of Group of Seven by Arthur Goss (Arts & Letters Club, Toronto); LAC. *Beyond a Reasonable Doubt*, 1956 (dir. Fritz Lang); Calgary Herald Archives. *Beyond a Reasonable Doubt*; found map. GMA; *I Want to Live!*, 1958 (dir. Robert Wise); *The Finger Points*, 1931 (dir. W.R. Burnett); *Yield to the Night*, 1956 (dir. J. Lee Thompson); *Caged*, 1950 (dir. John Cromwell).

Florence's Appeal

LAC (*Florence's Appeal*). Calgary Herald Archives; Edmonton Journal Archives; LAC; *The Paradine Case*, 1947 (dir. Alfred Hitchock). LAC. LAC.

Pic's Letter

GMA (*Pic's Letter*). GMA. GMA; *Angels with Dirty Faces*, 1938 (dir. Michael Curtiz).

The Execution

GMA (*The Execution*). *Without Sanctuary: Lynching Photography in America*, Santa Fe: Twin Palms, 2000 (2). Calgary Herald Archives; GMA (2).

La Tribuna Canadiana

GMA (*La Tribuna Canadiana*). LAC. LAC.

Back End Paper

GMA.

Back Cover

The Godfather Part II.

The Frank Iacobucci Centre, formerly the Centre for Italian Canadian Studies, was established in 1984 to promote research and publication on cultural and social aspects of the Italian Canadian community. Since 1988 the Centre has been located within the Department of Italian Studies of the University of Toronto. In 1995 the Centre was named after Justice Frank Iacobucci, the first Canadian of Italian origin to be appointed to the Supreme Court of Canada. The Centre encourages Canadian Italian studies in collaboration with local, national, and international organizations and through activities which include publication of the journal *Italian Canadiana*, the organization of conferences and lecture series aimed at involving the entire Italian Canadian community, and the creation of a digital archive documenting the Italian Canadian experience (www1.utoronto.ca/iacobucci/) and other databases.

Frank Iacobucci Centre
for Italian Canadian Studies
Department of Italian Studies,
University of Toronto
100 St. Joseph Street
Toronto ON M5S 1J4
www.utoronto.ca/iacobucci/